# The Beginner's Guide to Reloading Ammunition

### With Space and Money Saving Tips for Apartment Dwellers and Those on a Budget.

## By
## Steven Gregersen

The Second Amendment to the United States Constitution

*********

A well regulated militia being necessary to the security of a free state, the right of the people to keep and bear arms shall not be infringed.

**********

# The Beginner's Guide to Reloading

With space and money saving tips for apartment dwellers and those on a budget!

By Steven Gregersen

Copyright © Steven Gregersen

All rights reserved. Except for use in reviews, no part of this book may be reproduced or transmitted in any form without the written consent of the author.

## Disclaimer

The information contained here is based upon the author's experience and limited research. It is your responsibility to know and comply with any local, state, and federal laws that apply to you.

There is always a level of risk involved when reloading ammunition. Be safe. Never exceed the manufacturer's published load data. Always work up new loads with caution. Always consult up-to-date manuals for load data.

The information in this book is presented for academic study only. The author assumes no responsibility for its use.

# Table of Contents

Introduction - 9

Chapter One: Why reload your own ammunition? - 10

Chapter Two: Primers - 14

Chapter Three: Cases - 19

Chapter Four: Gunpowder - 42

Chapter Five: Bullets - 50

Chapter Six: Tools and Equipment - 64

Chapter Seven: The Process - 92

Chapter Eight: Reloading Shotgun Ammunition - 124

Chapter Nine: Safety - 145

Appendix - 148

# Introduction

Writing this book brings back a flood of memories. I've been reloading my own ammunition for over 40 years. I began with a Lee Loader virtually identical to the models sold today. I spent hours depriming, priming, resizing cases, pouring in the powder, and seating and crimping bullets for my Ruger Security Six 357 Magnum revolver. It was the only way I could afford to shoot the thing! Ammunition for magnum handguns was expensive then as now.

My reloading days were disrupted by a three year tour in the USMC then I was reloading again once I re-entered civilian life. For almost all of my adult life I've reloaded my own ammunition and for the majority of that time I've been casting my own bullets too.

As I said in a previous book, I don't consider myself an expert in much of anything but I've done enough reloading and teaching (many subjects) over the years to feel competent in instructing others.

My hope in writing this book is that you also experience some of the life-long joys of crafting your own ammunition.

# Chapter One: Why Reload Your Own Ammunition?

Everyone has their own reasons for reloading ammunition. When I began it was **to save money**. In 1971, Ruger came out with their Security Six, double action revolver in .357 Magnum and I couldn't wait to buy one. Even then, magnum handgun ammunition was expensive and I could easily make my own for half the cost of buying new.

For example: The purchase price of a box of 50, 158 grain, jacketed hollow point (JHP), .357 Magnum cartridges will set you back about $32.00 here. (Note: Ammunition prices fluctuate. The numbers quoted above reflect local costs on the day they were surveyed.) This is with reloadable, boxer primed, brass cases. That's about sixty-four cents per shot. It will cost about thirty-one cents each to reload those cases. If you have to purchase new brass cases for eighteen cents each your total cost to reload each cartridge will climb to forty-nine cents each. You can buy all new components and still spend fifteen cents less for each cartridge by making your own ammo. The brass can be reused many times so you can easily shoot for half the price of store-bought ammo.

If you're shooting magnum rifle ammo the savings are even higher. I can purchase *premium* cartridges with controlled expansion bullets for my .338 Winchester Magnum for about $2.85 each. I can make the home-grown equivalent for less than $1.25. That's a savings of $32.00 for a box of only *twenty* cartridges.

## Personal Satisfaction

But aside from the money saving there are other good reasons to "roll your own" ammo. From a very early age I've enjoyed making things and even more so as an adult. There's an intense satisfaction achieved when creating something from raw material so making my own ammunition is a rewarding experience.

## Customized Ammunition

I've already mentioned the cost savings of making your own premium ammunition compared to buying it. But there's far more than financial gain here. I live in elk and moose country. With good shot placement they aren't usually difficult to put down but they are large animals and you'll be more consistent with controlled expansion bullets. Now hear me out before you fire off that nasty review. I've killed elk and seen them killed using run-of-the-mill, store-bought ammunition. I've also seen some impressive bullet failures.

One in particular was on a large Whitetail buck. At the shot, the deer dropped like a rock but when I went to retrieve it there was a huge hole in its side. I thought at first it was an exit wound but then realized it was on the side facing me. The bullet had self-destructed on impact, blowing away hide, hair and meat on the rib cage. I did not find a single shred of lead inside the chest cavity but there were dozens of small bits and pieces on the hide and meat on the outside. What killed the deer were bone fragments from a couple of ribs that broke from the bullet's impact. The fragments acted like shrapnel, shredding the lungs and dropping the deer where it stood.

Ever since that day I've been a fan of controlled expansion bullets. (More about those later.)

But customized ammo is more than just fancy bullets. You can work up loads to get the maximum accuracy and velocity from your firearm or you can go the other way and make reduced loads for smaller shooters who want less recoil. Every firearm is unique in some ways with its own likes and dislikes. Most function quite well with factory ammo but if you like to get the ultimate from your firearm, rolling your own is a good place to begin.

## Availability

There are two aspects of availability: first, having ammo when the store shelves are empty, and second, loading for obsolete, obscure or other hard-to-find cartridges.

There are many old, yet serviceable firearms for which ammunition is no longer commercially available. Some of these can be put back into use through reloading and perhaps some minor case forming. I used to reload for my 7.5X55 Swiss rifle because new ammunition was scarce and/or prohibitively expensive. I was always able to find cases through Norma (ammunition manufacturer) but if that source dried up I could have made 7.5X55 cases from .284 Winchester cases.

After the presidential election in 2008, panic buying at home and wars in the Middle-East made loaded ammunition difficult to find. When you did find it the prices had shot through the ceiling. You could still find reloading components though and, for a while at least, the prices remained stable. Reloaders were virtually unaffected by the shortage for the first couple of years.

## Ammunition Restrictions

Some states in their misguided (and futile) attempts to limit criminal use of firearms contemplated limits on ammo purchases. It might sound reasonable to limit ammo sales to one or two boxes per day, week, or month but such efforts have no effect on criminal activity. They do, however, make it difficult to take advantage of ammo sales. As usual only the law-abiding firearm owners experience any inconvenience from such legislation. But if you reloaded your own ammo you were in luck. There are seldom any restrictions on purchasing ammunition components. If a sale was on, you could stock up while the prices were good then build up your stock of ammo at your leisure.

## Chapter Two: Primers

Primers are the ignition source that sets the gunpowder on fire. They aren't all alike! There are magnum and non-magnum primers, large pistol and large rifle primers and small pistol and small rifle primers. European and Asian countries use Berdan type primers while American manufacturers use Boxer primers. Shotgun primers are different in size and shape than primers for metallic cartridges. Some modern, "inline" muzzleloading firearm manufacturers recommend a milder shotgun type (209) primer for their firearms. Many of these variations have the same external dimensions and appearance but they are not interchangeable.

## Perhaps it would help to explain how a primer works.

A primer contains priming compound that explodes when impacted. The compound is found in the bottom of the metal outer cup. A boxer primer has an "anvil" that looks like a small, metal cone placed with the center resting on the priming mixture. When the primer is seated the wide part of the anvil is held in place by the back of the primer pocket. When the trigger is pulled the firing pin strikes the center, outside of the metal cup, crushing the priming compound between the metal cup and the raised center of the anvil which ignites the priming compound. The fire that results is channeled past the anvil's legs and into the powder through a hole in the center of the primer pocket. The fire ignites the gunpowder which then sends the bullet (or shot) down and out of the barrel.

Berdan primers function identically to Boxer primers but their construction is different. The "anvil" is machined into the primer pocket of the case and has two, smaller ports to channel the fire into the case.

Boxer and Berdan primers are not interchangeable!

# Rifle and Pistol Primers

I've lumped these together because they share some of the same attributes. First, the external dimensions of small rifle and small pistol primers are identical just as the dimensions of large rifle and large pistol primers are the same.

The problem is that even though they *look* identical they aren't!

The heaviest loadings in the 44 Magnum use only slightly more gunpowder than the smallest, center-fire rifle cartridges. The highest pressures generated in magnum handgun cartridges are still far below most mild pressured rifle cartridges. Handgun primers tend to be thinner than rifle primers because of this. Handgun primers also use less priming compound because they have less powder to ignite.

Of course one could wonder why not just use rifle primers in handguns. They would fit but the results might not be what you anticipated. First, the metal of a rifle primer is thicker and tougher than a handgun primer in order to withstand the higher pressures found in rifles. It's possible that the firing pin on a handgun wouldn't have enough force to fire the primer. Second, you normally get the best accuracy and consistency by using the mildest primer that still provides good ignition.

The difference between standard and magnum primers in both handguns and rifles is in the amount of priming compound. Magnum cartridges use more (and slower burning) powder than "regular" cartridges so they need a stronger ignition source.

Reloading manuals include the name and number of the primers they used in formulating their data. It's best to stay with their recommendations whenever possible. If for some reason you cannot, you should begin with the lowest (gunpowder) load level listed in the manual and work your way up by ½ grain increases until you have a safe, but satisfactory load. (Note: There'll be more about working up loads later.)

## Boxer vs. Berdan

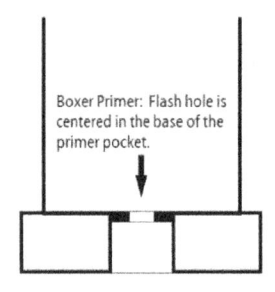

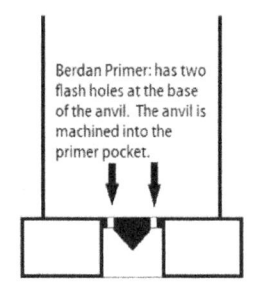

Boxer Primer: Flash hole is centered in the base of the primer pocket.

Berdan Primer: has two flash holes at the base of the anvil. The anvil is machined into the primer pocket.

I mentioned earlier that Americans use Boxer primers while the rest of the world uses Berdan primers. Again, they do not interchange. You must use the correct primer.

Boxer primers contain the shell, priming compound and anvil. Berdan primers have only the outer shell and priming compound. The anvil is machined into the primer pocket in the cartridge and instead of one large hole in the center of the primer pocket; there are two smaller holes - one on each side of the cone's base.

It's easier to remove a Boxer primer. You just push it out with a thin steel "decapping" pin during the reloading process.

Berdan primers are more difficult. To remove Berdan primers you can fill the case with liquid (usually water) then push a tight-fitting dowel in the case neck and whack it with a mallet. (Be sure to stand the cartridge case on a nut or stacked washers so that the primer has enough room to clear the case.) Water pressure will force the primer out of the case. With practice you can do it without making too big of a mess. The other method is to poke a hole in the primer then pry it out.

Once you have the primer out you'll need a new one to put back in. Boxer primers are easy to find in the United States. Berdan primers are a little more challenging!

## Shotgun Primers

Shotgun primers come in only one size (#209). Your choices when purchasing them is going to be limited to the manufacturer.

Many of the new, inline muzzleloading firearms use shotgun primers as an ignition source. Initially they used the same primers as those used in shot shells. But then they began to experiment and found that a milder primer gave them more accuracy. The result was shot shell size 209 primers made expressly for muzzleloading firearms. Even though these will fit in shot shell cases, they may not reliably ignite powder charge.

## Rim fire

The last priming system is called the rim fire.

Rim fire priming systems received the name because the liquefied priming compound is poured into the case where it settles into a gap around the rim of the case. When the trigger is pulled the firing pin strikes the outer case rim which pinches the priming compound, setting it off. Because the priming compound is already in the same chamber as the powder it ignites the powder directly. (There's no need to channel it through holes in the case.)

While they can be reloaded under dire circumstances the priming compound is not commercially available (you have to make your own!) so you'll seldom see it done.

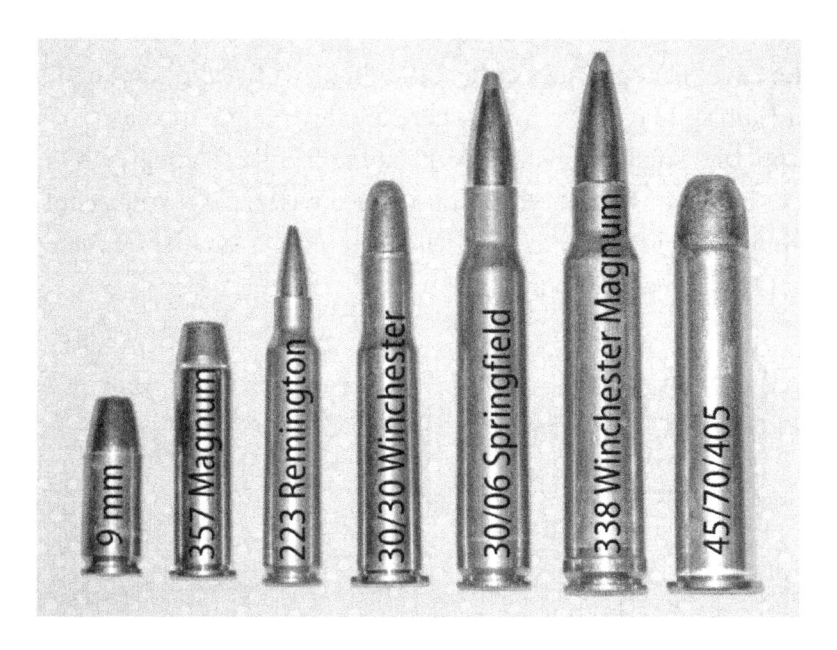

**The 9mm, 223, and 30/06 have "rimless" cases. The 357, 30/30 and 45/70 have "rimmed" cases. The 338 Winchester Magnum has a "belted" case.**

# Chapter 3: Cases

If you've done much shooting you've already noted that cartridge cases come in an assortment of sizes and shapes. There are straight walled cases like those used in most handguns and a few rifles. There are bottle necked cases that are most often seen in rifles but occasionally used in handguns. Some cases have projecting rims while "rimless" cases have rims the same diameter (or less) than the case.

Straight walled (rimmed) cases are the simplest designs and date back to the black powder days. They're still used in many handgun cartridges and a few rifle cartridges like the 45/70 and

444 Marlin. The 22 rim fire is another example of a straight walled, rimmed case.

Bottle-necked cases have a tapered "shoulder." The case is larger at the rear then continues either straight or with a slight reduction in size until it nears the front where the taper angle increases sharply to a small diameter "neck" at the front. The degree of taper varies considerably. Bottle-necked cases allow you to put more powder in a shorter case while shooting a smaller diameter bullet (to increase velocity).

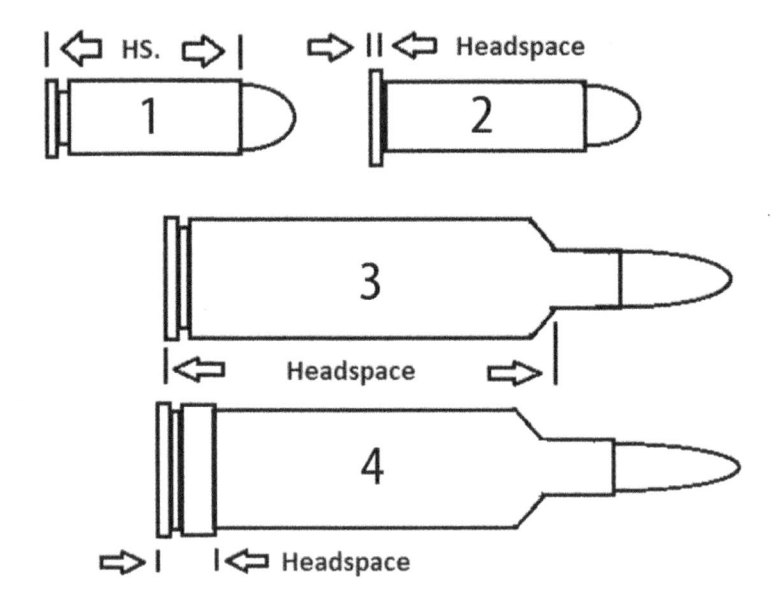

## Headspace

Headspace is the distance between the part of the chamber that stops the cartridge's forward motion and the front of the bolt face. The front edge of the case mouth stops forward motion on straight side, rimless cases (#1) like most of those used in semi-auto handguns. Rimmed and belted cases (#'s 2 & 4) are stopped by the forward edge of the rim or belt. Rimless, bottlenecked cases (#3) are stopped at the front portion of the bottleneck. Not shown are semi-rimmed cases (the "rim" is not as pronounced as "rimmed" cases), and rebated cases (a rimless case with the rim being smaller than the diameter of the cartridge's base).

When you pull the trigger and the firearm goes "bang" a lot of things happen in a very short time. When the firing pin hits the primer it slams the cartridge forward in the chamber. As the powder burns the hot gasses build up pressure. The pressure exerts itself equally in every direction. The bullet is gripped tightly by the case neck but the brass case can't stand a lot of pressure before something's got to give. As the pressure increases and the brass expands, the bullet gets its freedom and makes a hasty exit down the barrel. In the meantime the gasses are still expanding and building up pressure. The case expands quickest at the front where the brass is thinnest. The front of the case actually wedges itself tight in the chamber. The expansion continues as the pressure builds but since the front can't move, the case stretches to the rear until it's stopped by the bolt face. If this distance is too great the case may actually separate or pull itself apart. In extreme conditions it may allow hot, high pressure gasses to escape causing physical damage to the firearm and the shooter.

Headspace is deemed excessive when it exceeds standards set by firearms and cartridge manufacturers. Due to the machining and fitting process, manufacturers have both minimum and maximum acceptable chamber dimensions. The 30/06, for example allows .006 inch difference between the shortest and longest chamber lengths. Cartridge manufacturers must size cases small enough to fit the minimum chamber dimension but they too are allowed .006 inch for manufacturing processes. So if the chamber is at the maximum length and the cartridge is the minimum length you may have .012 inch of headspace and still be within limits. Now, if you reload that ammunition and squeeze that case down just a bit too far and your rifle's had a few thousand rounds shot through it and the chamber is just a little loose you've got a recipe for disaster ...

(which leads us to the next point!)

**Excessive headspace can occur in either the firearm or, the ammunition.**

Dies or shell holders that are worn or improperly machined may push the shoulder back too far when resizing cases which will create excessive headspace where there was none before. If you trim straight side, rimless cases too short you'll also create excessive headspace (because they set the headspace on the cases' mouth).

If you want to cover all of your bases, you can purchase *case* headspace gauges from many reloading equipment manufacturers. You drop the cartridge in the gauge to tell if it's too long or too short.

If you suspect that the headspace in the gun is off take it to a gunsmith who'll use machined, "go," "no-go," and "field" gauges to check its headspace.

**Look for shiny "rings" or cracks around the case when inspecting cases for separation. Usually they're near the rim but may be farther up the case.**

For most firearm owners the first indications of excessive headspace come when fired cases separate or become difficult to extract. *If you have cases separating (especially with new cases), stop shooting the firearm and get its headspace checked.*

*Difficult extraction should also be taken very seriously.* A fired case should take only slightly more effort to extract than it did to chamber. I've seen people hit the bolt handle with a 2X4 trying to extract a fired case then immediately shoot the firearm again. That's really stupid!

## Case Preparation

Case preparation is what you do to make a case ready for reloading with new components. Some things are safety issues, some are practical issues (won't work if you don't do it!) and some are cosmetic. With each heading I'll tell you if this is something you should do always or just do as needed.

I've included a quick reference below showing which steps should always be done and which should be done only as needed. More detailed instructions for each process are in the text below.

### Cartridge Case Preparation

| Process | Always | As Needed | Notes |
|---|---|---|---|
| Inspection | * | | |
| Deprime/Prime | * | | |
| Resize | * | | May be either neck, full-length or small-base. |
| Cleaning | | * | |
| Trimming | | * | |
| Chamfer/Deburr | | * | |
| Neck Diameter | | * | |
| Primer Pocket | | * | Clean, chamfer or swage as needed. |
| Annealing | | * | Anneal only the case neck, not the entire case! |
| Crimping | | * | See the specific instructions in the text! |

# Inspection (Always)

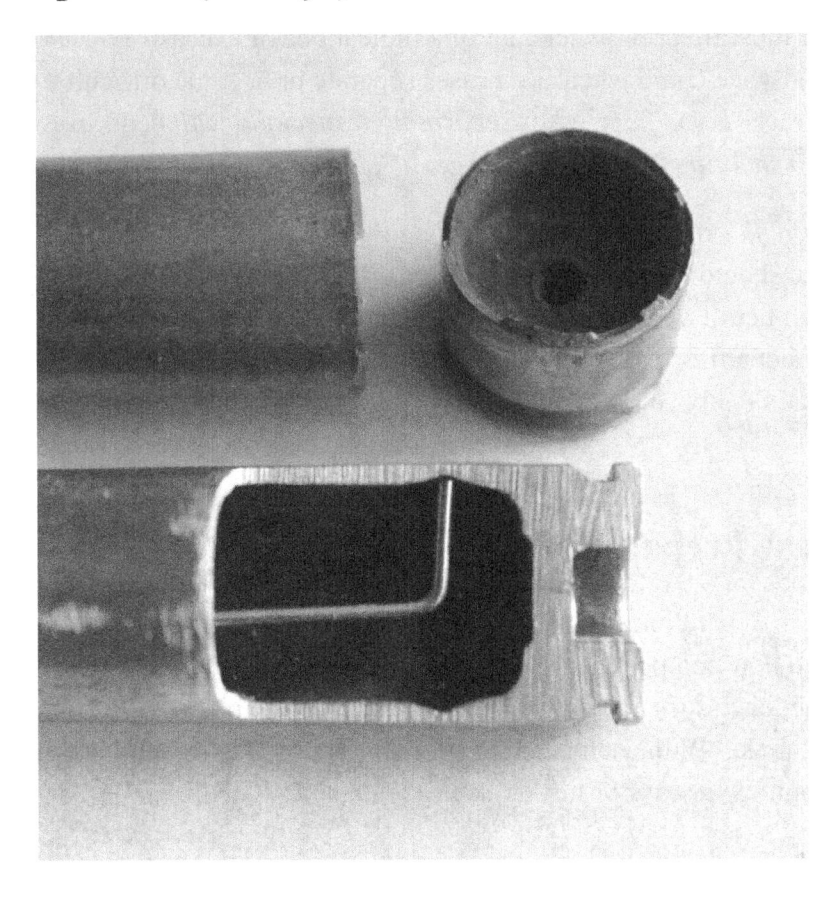

**I use a bent paper clip to probe the inside of bottleneck cases for thin spots that are the beginning of case separation. The interior of the case should smoothly taper from the head to the shoulder. If the paper clip hangs up or I feel a groove inside the case I crush the case with pliers and trash it.**

Every case should be inspected prior to being reloaded. Look over the outside for evidence of cracks, splits and case separation.

Always inspect the primer for signs of leakage around the edges or for a punctured primer. Both of these can be signs of excessive pressure which can expand the primer pocket to the point that a new primer won't stay seated.

Cases that have been reloaded several times sometimes develop cracks in the neck (on bottleneck cartridges) or mouth (straight wall cases) because these areas are worked the most.

Check carefully for signs of case separation. Sometimes the only indication will be a thin bright line or ring visible on the outside of the case.

## Depriming and Priming (Always)

Obviously you'll need to remove the spent primer prior to installing a new one. They usually come out easily unless you're working with surplus military brass with crimped in primers. (The military crimps their primers to keep them in place when firing on full-auto.) Keep a few extra depriming pins on hand when depriming military cases because you'll probably break some before you're done.

When you remove a crimped primer there will be a sharp edge around the primer pocket. Use a deburring (or chamfering) tool or the point of a knife to cut off the sharp edge and chamfer it slightly. Otherwise when you seat a new primer it will catch on the edge of the pocket and possibly be deformed when seating it.

While you have the primer out you might want to clean the primer pocket. There'll always be some ash residue around the flash hole. There are special tools for this or you can just scrape it out with a small, flat type screwdriver blade. I little bit of residue won't hurt anything but if it's thick a section can break off and block the flash hole when you seat the new primer. Blocking the flash hole can cause a misfire (the firearm does not go off) or a hang fire (the firearm discharges several seconds after pulling the trigger).

# Resizing (Always)

When you shoot a firearm the pressure expands the cartridge case. When resizing the case you run it through a "die" that's shaped like (but slightly smaller than) the chamber of your firearm. This squeezes the cartridge case back to its original dimensions. Otherwise it might be too big to fit back into the chamber.

There are three types of sizing dies available: Neck, Full Length, and Small Base.

**Neck Sizing**

A neck sizing die can be used with bottleneck cartridges to squeeze the neck of the cartridge (the front part that grips the bullet) back to its original size. The rest of the case is not changed. Neck sizing has its good and bad points.

The good points are that case life is extended because you're not working the brass as much. Full-length resizing squeezes the brass case back to its original dimensions but, most of the compaction happens in the front third of the case. When you fire it again the same process happens in which the front of the brass grips the chamber making the brass case stretch backwards to contact the bolt face. In each occurrence, the case gets a little thinner at the back. Eventually the case will separate even if the firearm's headspace is correct. When you neck size the case the only part being squeezed back to size is the neck. Thus, since the case is already the same size as the chamber, the only part stretching upon firing is the neck. Eventually the brass in the neck will get brittle and split. But, you'll be able to use the case much longer before that happens and if you anneal and trim the case regularly you'll get even longer life out of it.

Accuracy may also be improved when neck sizing because the case fits the chamber tighter, meaning there's less movement of the cartridge in the chamber. This keeps everything lined up more consistently from shot to shot.

There are some problems you may experience by only neck sizing cases.

First, you will probably not be able to use those cartridges in any other firearm. If you have only one firearm in that caliber it won't be an issue. If you have more than one you'll have to mark and separate the ammo for each gun.

A second problem is that some cases may be more difficult to chamber and may stick when trying to extract them without firing them first. To avoid problems when hunting you'll want to individually chamber and extract each cartridge you plan on taking with you. Leave the oversize cartridges at home to be used in the practice range.

Third: Neck sized cartridges may not work well in anything except bolt action rifles. That's because bolt actions have a "camming" effect that increases your leverage when you open and close the bolt. They can actually force a slightly oversize case into the chamber. If you have other action types you should probably full length resize your cases.

**Full Length Resizing**

A full length die squeezes the entire case back to factory dimensions so that it will fit in any properly head spaced chamber. Always use a good case lube when full-length sizing cases. Otherwise you run the danger of the case sticking in the die and pulling the rim off the case when you try to get it back out. The exception is when sizing straight sided cases with *some* carbide dies. *Some* of these work without lubricating the cases. Check the instructions that came with the die. (But even those that can be used without case lube work better if you lube the case!)

The best point about full length sizing is that the cartridges can be used in *most* firearms. That's a bonus if you have different firearms using the same cartridge. Accuracy is generally good.

The biggest detriment to full length sizing is case life. That's a lot of stretching and squeezing which hardens the brass and makes case elongation a bigger issue. You can anneal the case necks to alleviate splits but even then case life is considerably shorter when full length sizing the cases.

**Small Base Resizing**

Small base sizing is like full length resizing with an attitude! Small base dies go a step beyond full length dies by squeezing down the base of the cartridge to *minimum* factory dimensions. It's seldom needed unless you shoot a military look-alike rifle such as an AR-15. Many of these rifles have no camming action when the bolt closes and cannot chamber a cartridge that's even slightly oversize. If you reload for an AR-15 or similar, semi-automatic rifle you may want to invest in and use a set of small base dies.

# Cleaning (As Needed)

Cases need cleaned if they're dirty. Otherwise they'll scratch up the inside of your dies. I've picked up range brass (brass lying on the ground at popular shooting areas) that was covered in dirt and mud. I usually dump them in a pan filled with dish soap and water, stir them up occasionally while they soak, then dump the soapy water and rinse the cases with clean water. I stand them upright and let them dry in the sun (in the summer), or behind the wood stove if it's winter time.

If the brass is tarnished I'll put them in a tumbler or vibrating case cleaner with the proper medium and run it until they look like new again.

Lee Precision makes shell holders that go in an electric drill. You clamp in the cartridge and spin it using the drill's motor while you polish the outside with fine steel wool or sandpaper. This works well for heavily tarnished brass in small batches.

If the brass is corroded toss it.

**Lyman Case Trimmer**

# Trimming (As Needed)

Case length is serious business. Every time you discharge a firearm a minute amount of brass flows forward causing the case to stretch. Over time it all adds up and the cases must be trimmed back to specifications. In its severest form the mouth of the case can be jammed against the front of the rifle's chamber. That crimps the end of the case tightly against the bullet, pinching it in place, so that when it's fired the case cannot expand to release the bullet. The result can be disastrous.

Another reason to trim cases is to square the ends. Many times the factory crimp in a case is so severe that, after firing, the case mouth is noticeably uneven. Although it may not be stretched enough to be unsafe it may affect accuracy. If the case mouth is not square the bullet will drag on the long side as it leaves the cartridge. If the barrel's throat is even slightly oversized the bullet may enter the rifling at an angle or off-center. That's going to destroy accuracy!

*Incidentally, "throat" refers to the section of the rifle's bore that's between the front of the chamber and where the rifling begins. The distance may vary. It's sometimes called "free bore."*

Long cases may show up during the bullet seating or crimping process. The case will contact the crimping ring in the die and be pushed back; buckling the case (straight wall cartridges), or it may buckle the shoulder on bottle neck cartridges. I once had a problem with an occasional 357 magnum cases buckling when I crimped the case to the bullet. I checked case length and ended up trimming the entire batch of 300 (plus!) to get the cases to crimp consistently.

Most reloading manuals list the maximum case length at the front of the section on reloading that particular cartridge.

You can use a case length gauge or calipers to measure the case.

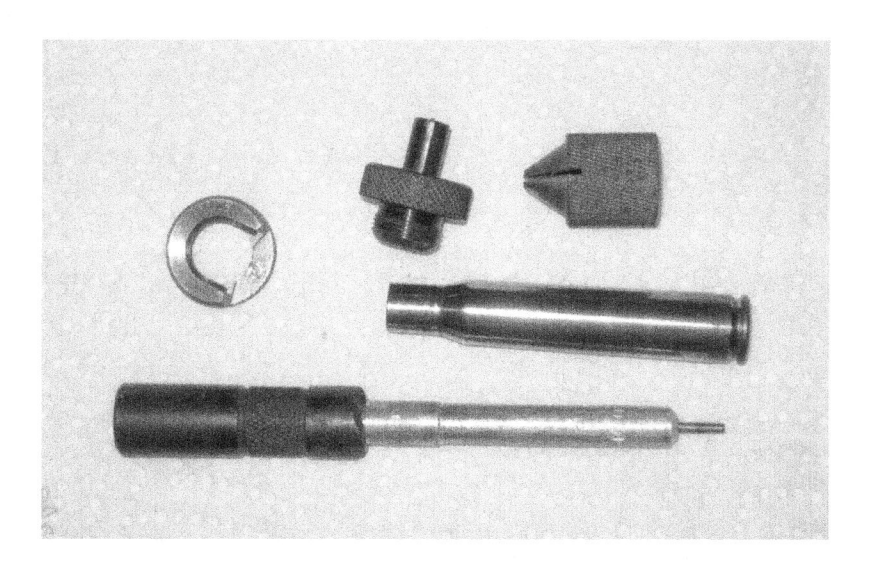

**This is a Lee case length gauge, shell holder, trimmer and chamfer tool along with a 30/06 case that's been polished, trimmed and chamfered.**

Another option is to purchase a Lee Precision Cutter and Lock Stud along with a Lee Case Length Gauge and Shell Holder. These measure and trim your cases at the same time. It would take a little longer than just measuring the cartridges but if they're too long you could also trim them then.

Case stretching is not normally a problem until after a case has been reloaded many times but I've occasionally seen once-fired cases that needed to be trimmed. It's something you need to be aware of.

**Here I'm using the Lee chamfer tool and a drill to deburr a case after trimming.**

## Deburring/Chamfering (As Needed)

When you trim a case the edges will have sharp corners and small shards of brass hanging from them. These make it difficult to start bullets. The remedy is to cut them off and bevel the edges with a chamfering tool. You can purchase specially made tools for the job or use a sharp knife (and caution!)

Even if you didn't trim the case, chamfering the mouth will make it easier to start the bullet into the case.

## Neck Diameter (As Needed)

As the cartridge case becomes a little longer each time you fire it, it also becomes a little thicker. That's because every time you torch off a round a minute amount of the brass in the case "flows" forward. When you trim the length of a case you cut off the front part of the case but you do nothing about the thickness of the case walls. The flowing brass keeps accumulating until the case neck is so thick that its diameter is too big for the chamber. The effect is the same as an overly long case. The bullet is gripped tightly because the case cannot expand enough to let it go after you pull the trigger.

The remedy is reaming out the case neck to reduce its thickness. Lee does not (to my knowledge) offer any tools for this job. You can get case neck reamers from reloading equipment manufacturers like RCBS, Lyman, and Forrester. The best kind have a mandrel that the case neck slides over then the case is thinned by a lathe type cutter that removes the excess brass from the outside of the case.

You'll need a way to measure the outside diameter of the case neck. Dial calipers (or regular calipers if you have good eyes!) or a micrometer can do the job.

## Primer Pocket (As Needed)

Before you clean, deprime or reload any cases inspect the primer for signs of leakage. Typically if a primer pocket is enlarged by excessive pressures (or poor machining) you'll see dark lines around its circumference. Another thing to watch for is punctured primers. A punctured primer results when pressure inside the case blows a hole where the firing pin impacted the primer. The excess pressure may or may not deform the primer pocket.

Look at the flash hole while you have the primer out. It should be round and unobstructed. I've seen a few that were obviously undersized and/or otherwise misshapen.

When you seat the new primer be sure it will stay in place. There should be some resistance. If there's too much resistance the primer may be deformed or, in severe cases, fire while you are installing it. Be especially cautious when using a Lee Classic reloader.

## Annealing (As Needed)

Annealing should be considered when case necks begin to crack or when you see soot on the front of the case after firing. (This may be caused by the case neck not expanding in the chamber to seal off combustion gasses.)

Annealing is a process in which the neck of the cartridge is heated to restore elasticity. Brass becomes "work hardened" and brittle by the constant stretching and compaction that happens when the cases are fired then resized. Eventually it become so brittle that the necks crack, making the case unsuitable for reloading. Brittle brass also makes the resizing process (especially expanding the neck), more difficult and can affect accuracy because the case neck's tension on the bullet is too great.

Annealing brass extends case life up to ten times and makes neck tension more consistent. Only the case's neck should be annealed. *Note: The brass of a cartridge case is supposed to be hard at the base to contain the pressure generated by firing the gun. If you anneal the entire case you'll soften the base as well and then you're asking for trouble.*

The procedure to anneal cases is simple yet exacting. First the brass must be above 485 degrees Fahrenheit before any changes can take place. If the temperature never reaches that point nothing is changed and nothing is gained. You want to heat the case neck and upper shoulder area to a temperature of approximately 700 to 800 degrees Fahrenheit (while keeping the lower 2/3 of the case below 485 degrees). At this temperature the brass will begin to discolor. Forget about heating it to a dull red or orange as some recommend. By then you've gone too far. Over-annealing the *neck area* does not create a dangerous situation but there are negative results. The brass will lose its elasticity and you may notice that extracting the spent case is slightly more difficult. There may be a reduction in accuracy as well.

About the only small scale method I'd recommend is holding the cartridge by the base with your bare fingers while heating the neck with a propane torch. You'll need to rotate the case to ensure even heating all around the neck. If the case gets too hot to hold or the case neck begins to change color drop it in a pan of water. Quenching brass does not make it hard or brittle as it does steel. All you're doing is cooling it down quickly to ensure that the base doesn't overheat.

Properly annealed necks will have a slight color change and maintain a dull shine. If the shine is gone the brass was overheated.

There are other methods people use such as heating cases that are standing in a pan of water but overheating can be a problem with most of them. The water method keeps the base cool (which is good!) but often results in getting the necks too hot. The finger method is the safest way because it ensures that you won't overheat the base of the cartridge. Annealing the base is something you truly want to avoid!

There are machines that produce more consistent results if you want to spend the money. I wouldn't advise it unless you get into reloading a lot of ammunition. If you are neck sizing cartridges and not shooting maximum loads you should get at least ten reloads per case.

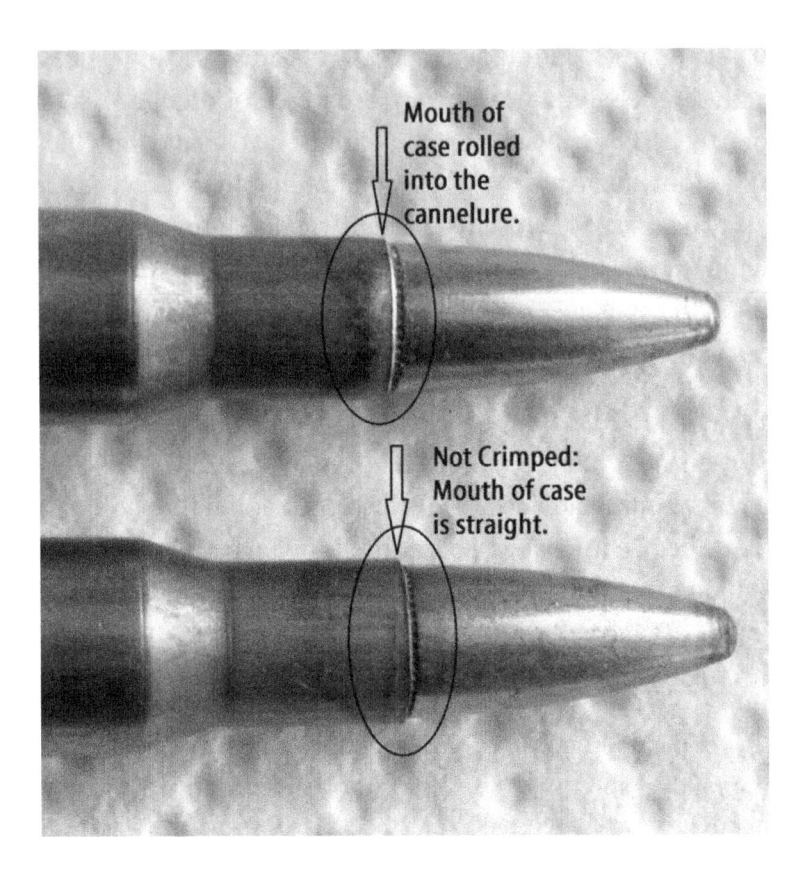

Mouth of case rolled into the cannelure.

Not Crimped: Mouth of case is straight.

## Crimping (As Needed)

Crimping refers to squeezing the brass at the case mouth against the bullet to help hold it in place. Many manufacturers crimp their bullets in place because they have no control over how the ammo will be treated and what type of firearm it will be used in. Be aware that crimping shortens case life. I don't do it unless I need to.

The three most common crimp options for the reloader are:

- The "Roll Crimp" – this is what most dies come with. It rolls the case mouth into the crimp groove (cannelure) on the bullet. This is my favorite for lead bullets. ***Only bullets with a cannelure or crimp groove should be roll crimped.*** (The crimp should be *in* the cannelure, *not* above or below it.)
- The "Taper Crimp" – this one squeezes the case mouth tight on the bullet. These hold very tightly but you have to be careful applying them. It's very easy to get one too tight and deform the bullet without knowing it. It's not a highly visible crimp like the roll crimp or factory crimp. Taper crimps will work on bullets with or without a cannelure.
- The "Factory Crimp" - using factory crimp dies, are acceptable if done correctly. They can also be used on jacketed bullets that don't have a cannelure.

Crimping is one of those things that's needed in some applications, optional in others and not recommended in some. So, when should you crimp the bullet to the case? That depends on the cartridge, firearm and crimp type.

**Straight Walled, Rimless Cases**

***Use caution when crimping straight walled, rimless cases like those used in semi-automatic handguns.*** These use the front of the case to establish headspace.

- Roll Crimps should not be used on straight sided, rimless cases. If the case is roll crimped the cartridge could slide too far forward in the chamber, pinching the bullet and creating dangerously high pressure.
- Taper Crimps are acceptable if done correctly.
- "Factory Crimps" using factory crimp dies are acceptable if done correctly.
- Crimping may not be needed at all. I've never crimped

cartridges for my .45 Auto or 9 mm and I've never experienced problems as a result.

## Firearms with Tubular Magazines

*Always crimp the case on ammunition used in firearms with tubular magazines to* keep the bullet from being pushed into the case by the cartridge in front of it.

## Revolver Cartridges

*Always crimp revolver cartridges* to hold the bullet in place against recoil. Otherwise the bullets tend to "walk forward" out of the case.

## Semi and Fully Automatic Rifles

*Always crimp cartridges being used in semi or fully automatic rifles.* The first reason is that the cycling of the action slams the cartridges forward and backward in the magazine, beating them against the front and back of the magazine. I've had crimped bullets in steel cases pushed backwards into the cartridge case under these conditions. The second reason is that the speed of the action closing can actually pull a loose, fitting bullet forward and out of the case when the cartridge seats in the chamber. It's the inertia thing! The cartridge is slammed forward then stops suddenly. If the tension of the case neck and the crimp aren't strong enough the bullet will keep going after the case stops. If it's severe enough it will drive the bullet into the rifling. If the shooter quickly chambers another round and fires it without checking the bore it's most likely going to blow the rifle apart. Obviously that's something we'd prefer to avoid.

## Bottleneck Cartridges Used in Box Magazines

*Crimping is acceptable but not required on bottleneck cartridges used in box magazines.* Here it's to prevent the bullet from being driven backwards in the case by recoil. When the rifle fires the recoil slams it backwards into your shoulder. The cartridges in the magazine want to remain stationary so, in essence, they stay in the same place while the rifle (and magazine box) head for the rear. The cartridges then slam into the front of the magazine. This is why you'll see soft point bullets in the magazine with the tips flattened or otherwise deformed after you've fired a couple of shots. In severe instances it can also drive the bullets backwards into the case.

This most often happens in the larger calibers because the bullets and cartridges weigh more. I've heard of Professional Hunters in Africa doing herd control having this problem. They're usually shooting dangerous game with very large rifles. Instead of emptying the magazine then reloading they'll stop shooting with one round left in the magazine, they then reload the rifle and continue shooting. Saving the last round is a safety measure to keep from having an empty magazine in case a critter tries to kill them. After several cycles they found that the bullet in the bottom cartridge had been shoved back into the case. A bullet that is seated too deeply as in this situation will cause very high pressure when it is fired. It may be as deadly as the critter that's charging them.

*The caution here is that when you are shooting your rifle be sure to rotate the cartridges in the magazine so that one isn't taking the brunt of the damage.* Another reason to rotate the cartridges is that deformed bullets don't fly true. When I'm target shooting I load only one cartridge at a time to avoid this problem.

**Single Shot and Break Action Firearms**

There's seldom a reason to crimp the bullets in cartridges to be used in single shot firearms, double rifles, combination guns, etc.

# Military Case Preparation

Military surplus ammunition is often available at good prices and some of it is reloadable if you take a few things into account. First, the cases are often thicker which is good and bad. The good thing is that case life is often better than civilian versions. The bad thing is that you need to work up separate loads for military surplus brass. (You should work up new loads each time you change components.) Differences in case thickness change case volume which also changes the pressure in the case. Most of the time it's not a problem but it only takes one bad cartridge to cause irreparable damage to you and your firearm. Don't take chances. Shortcuts aren't worth the risk involved!

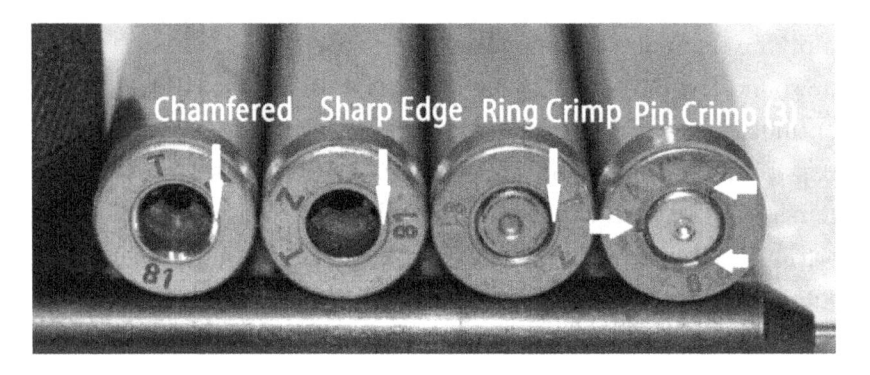

**These are military surplus cases with crimped primers. From left to right you'll see a primer pocket with the primer removed and the edges chamfered (or beveled); next is one with the primer removed but the edge is not beveled; next you'll see the primer held in the case with a ring crimp; the last one shows the primer held by a pin crimp.**

Surplus cases have crimped primers. These can be a challenge to remove. I keep extra decapping pins on hand because I often break some when decapping military brass.

Many manufacturers offer lifetime guarantees on decapping rods (not pins – the rod holds the pin), but you need to understand that a lifetime warranty doesn't mean they never break. It only means they'll replace it for free when it does break! I have a (lifetime guaranteed) universal depriming die made by RCBS. I've broken several decapping rods on military primers. Some primers were crimped in so tightly that the pin pushed through the primer but did not remove it. RCBS has always offered outstanding service for the decapping die or any of their products. When I need replacement parts I call them up, tell them what I need, and they drop it in the mail ...postage paid.

Once you have the primer removed you'll need to chamfer the primer pocket to cut out the crimp. You can use the point of a knife or buy a chamfering tool. If you're going to do many I'd advise investing in the tool! It's much faster.

**Removing Berdan Primers**

Be aware that some surplus brass is Berdan primed. To remove these you'll need to fill the case with water then push a tight fitting dowel or rod into the neck and rap it with a mallet. The hydraulic pressure will force the primer out of the case. You can also poke hole in the primer and pry it out with strong pick of some type. Some manufacturers sell tools for removing Berdan primers.

It's a more tedious process than removing Boxer primers and you'll need to locate a supply of Berdan primers to prime the cases with. Additionally, many of these cartridge cases are made of steel. They can be resized but it takes more effort.

Always check the case length of surplus brass. I've seen some that the crimp on the case mouth was so severe it stretched the brass.

# Chapter Four: Gunpowder

I had a friend who was a novice reloader. He bought a break open action, single shot handgun in a wildcat cartridge so factory ammo was not available. He immediately began experiencing problems with the firearm. When fired it would frequently release the barrel catch and eject the spent cartridge. He took the gun and some of his reloaded ammunition to the store where he purchased it. They pulled the bullets in several of his hand loads and weighed the powder charges. Many of them were well over the maximum safe charge. It turned out that he was using an adjustable powder measure that wasn't throwing consistent charges. He changed his reloading practices and the problem went away.

Don't take chances with gunpowder.

If you are having problems and take your firearm to a gunsmith bring some of the ammo you've been shooting. If they're reloads he's probably going to disassemble a few to do some measuring.

This is no place to let pride interfere with common sense. If you're doing something wrong or you have faulty equipment you need to find out before any permanent damage occurs to your firearm or you!

Smokeless (gun) powder is one of those things that looks simple, but isn't. Get a good reloading manual and do not deviate from it.

Smokeless powder is designed to function within narrow parameters and becomes unstable if used outside those limits. By unstable I mean that the pressures generated go beyond safe boundaries. *This is true using either too much or too little gunpowder.* In essence, if you use the wrong type of powder or the wrong amount of the "right" powder you aren't just reloading your ammunition, *you're making a bomb*.

In reloading circles you'll hear people talk of slow or fast "burn rates." What they're referring to is how fast the powder burns. Knowing burn rates is important when you work up your own loads from scratch. Handguns and shotguns use fast burning powder while the large magnum rifle cartridges use slow burning powder. I'm not getting too technical on this issue since this book is geared toward novices. Those new at reloading are better served by following the guidelines in the manual than in attempting to build a safe and effective load from scratch. I have resources listed in the appendix for those who want to learn more.

## Special Loads

Some reloading manuals and websites have loading specs for special loads such as shot loads for handguns or for loading over and/or underweight projectiles. Some reloaders use buckshot instead of "normal" bullets for reduced loads in rifles and handguns. The purpose is usually for shooting small game or cheap practice sessions. You may also find loading data for wax "bullets" that are sometimes used for shooting in indoor ranges or competitions. One manual I have lists separate loads for snub-nose revolvers because some powders perform better than others in short barrels.

If you're into this kind of reloading shop around until you find the data you need. Do not, as an amateur, try to work up your own loads without help from experienced and knowledgeable reloaders. As I've said before: you must match the powder to the load. It can be just as hazardous to use too little smokeless powder as it is to use too much.

## Grains *vs.* Ounces

Gun powder is measured by the "grain" instead of ounces or grams. We are not talking about one *granule* of powder. *Grain* is a measurement of weight. One pound (16 oz.) is equal to 7,000 grains. One ounce is equal to 437.5 grains. Get a good powder scale. A postal scale or your kitchen food scale just won't do the job!

## Reloading Manuals

Reloading manuals can sometimes seem contradictory. You'd think that with something as potentially hazardous as loading ammunition that there'd be more consistency in the load data they publish.

For example: The *maximum load* for the 30/06 cartridge firing a 180 grain soft point bullet and using WW760 (Winchester Western brand) is listed at 53.0 grains in the Winchester reloading guide

(2001). The *Speer* reloading manual (#12, 1995) lists the *maximum* 30/06, 180 gr. SP, load using WW760 at 55.0 grains and recommends using a CCI magnum primer.

So what's going on?

**Case volume makes a difference.**

A case with a smaller internal volume (meaning the brass is thicker as in military surplus cartridges) will have higher pressures than a thinner walled, higher volume, case manufactured for the civilian market.

**The bullet makes a difference.**

The bearing surface on bullets of the same size and weight but from different manufacturers may not be the same which changes the amount of friction generated by the bullet as it travels down the barrel. Even the thickness and composition of the bullet jacket or whether it has a lead or copper core will change things.

**The barrels make a difference.**

The bore finish, the rate of twist and even rifling differences (# of lands/grooves, polygonal rifling, etc.) will affect pressure and velocity. Barrel length has a striking effect on velocity.

**The primers make a difference.**

Primer manufacturer and power levels (magnum or standard) impact the velocity and pressure of the fired round.

In short, no two firearms or cartridges are exactly alike. Hence, the results will always differ.

**Always use the exact powder listed in the reloading manual.**

For example; Load data for H4350 (manufactured by Hodgdon Powder Co. Inc.) and IMR 4350 (a different brand of powder that's also manufactured by Hodgdon Powder Co. Inc.) are not interchangeable.

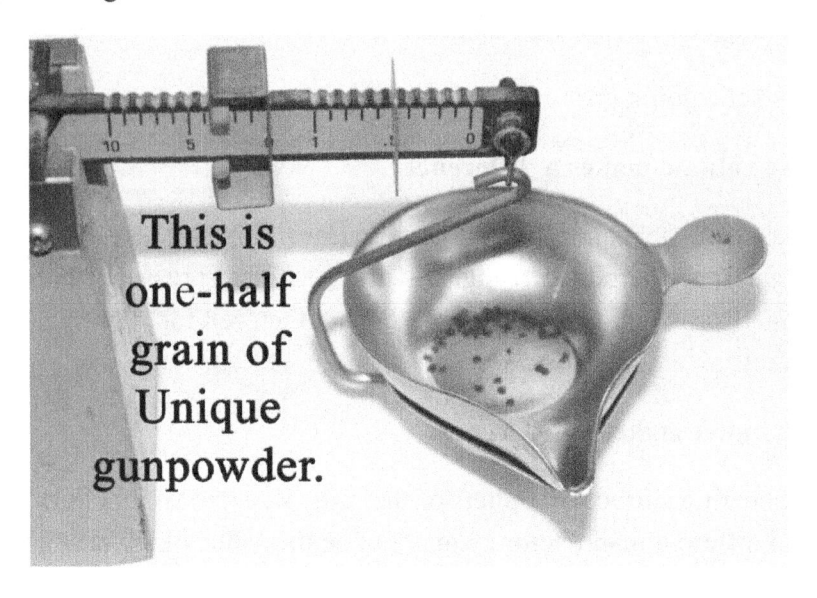

This is one-half grain of Unique gunpowder.

**Always work up new loads with caution.**

*A load is "new" any time you change a component.* That means if you switch from Federal cartridge cases to Remington cartridge cases you should start at the minimum powder level shown in the manual and increase it in .5 (one-half) grain steps until you reach the maximum load listed in the manual or you begin seeing signs of excessive pressure. If there is no minimum load listed in the manual, reduce the maximum listed charge weight by ten-percent for a starting load and work your way up from there.

If you switch bullet brands (with the same weight), or even primers, start over at a minimum level and work upwards by .5 grain increments.

*Always examine the cartridge case after each .5 grain increase.* If there are *any* signs of excessive pressure stop immediately and back the charge weight down at least one grain to where there are no indications of excessive pressure. Remember, every firearm is different. What constitutes a safe load in one may not be safe in another. It is not unusual to begin seeing signs of high pressure at charge levels below the maximums listed in the manuals. Don't go any farther.

**Some powders work better in bulk measurements than others.**

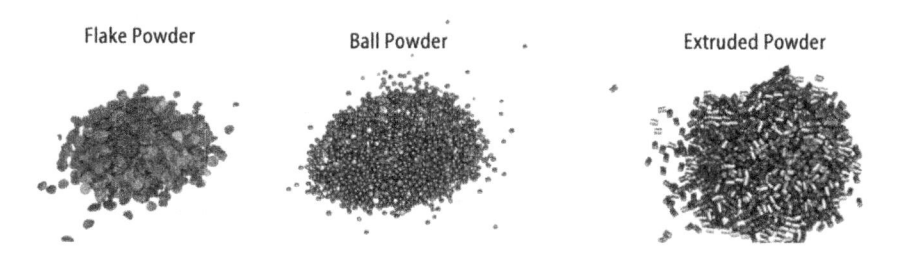

Flake Powder　　　　Ball Powder　　　　Extruded Powder

**(Left to right) Red Dot, WW760, IMR 4320**

Gunpowder comes in different shapes: flake, ball, and extruded. Flake powder is most commonly found in shotguns and handguns. Ball powder may be used in shotguns, handguns and rifles, while extruded powder is found most often in center fire rifle cartridges.

*Ball powder is the most consistent when used with bulk powder measures* simply because it has the finest granulation. Extruded powders do not work as well with bulk tools when measuring small amounts because of their large size but seems to be pretty consistent in the large cartridges. Flake powder does okay with bulk measures even with its large (relatively speaking) size.

I seldom load cartridges to the maximum amount. Maximum loads shorten case life and are hard on the guns and the shooter. The most accurate loads are usually arrived at before you reach maximum pressures anyway and the critter receiving the bullet can't tell the difference between a fast and not-quite-as-fast bullet at normal hunting ranges.

I always weigh maximum loads on a scale for safety concerns. I've seen what happens when a rifle or shotgun blows up and I want nothing to do with that.

I also try to choose powders that fill the case at least half way on a minimum load. That way, if a case is double charged it's obvious.

## Signs of Excessive Pressure

The primer has "flowed" into the cavity around the ejector rod.

Note the sharp corners on the primer. They should be "rounded off."

The indent where the firing pin struck the primer is "blown out". The gray color is from escaping powder gasses.

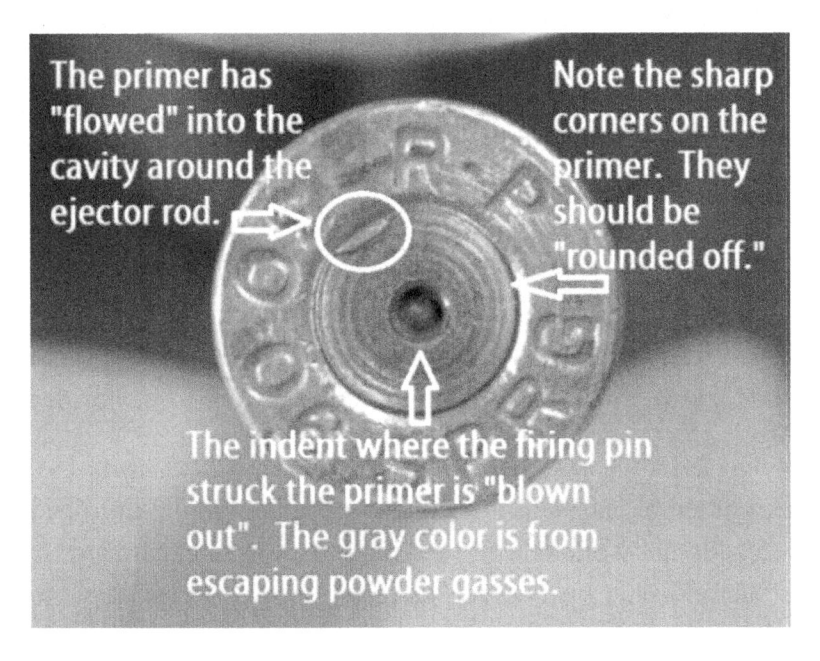

The symptoms listed below may or may not be signs of excessive pressure but until you've achieved "graduate level" in reloading you should take them seriously. *If you see any of these symptoms stop shooting immediately and have the firearm and loads checked by a competent gunsmith.*

*Primer cratering (metal flows back around the firing pin hole).

*Difficult extraction.

*Flattened Primer

*Expanded primer pocket (Look for signs of gas leakage around the edges of the primer or loose primers.)

*Gas leakage around the primer

*Blown Primer (hole blown through the primer, usually where the firing pin struck the primer)

*Excessive or unusually hard recoil

*Head Expansion (You'll need a micrometer for measuring this. You'll probably have an expanded primer pocket for additional evidence.)

*Short case life.

*Do not take chances with gunpowder.* Always use the exact gunpowder listed in the reloading manual. Never exceed the maximum charge levels shown in the manual. Any time you change even a single component, begin all over again by working up charge levels by ½ grain increments from the minimum listed in the manual.

Inspect every fired cartridge for evidence of excessive pressure. At the first sign of excessive pressure back off to a safe load level. If you are having problems take the firearm, some of your reloaded ammunition, plus your dies and shell holder to a competent gunsmith and have him check things over.

Reloading ammunition is inherently dangerous. If you are going to err, err on the side of caution.

# Chapter Five: Bullets

With the exception of safe loading practices, bullets are the most important choice for the reloader. You can do everything else perfectly but if the bullet is inferior it will never fly true. If you're shooting at a living animal not only must accuracy be good, the performance of the bullet upon impact is also critical. To add to the mix, some bullets won't work well in some firearms.

I've included a list of common bullet abbreviations found in reloading manuals. This is not an exhaustive list. You'll find that manuals published by bullet manufacturers will sometimes use different abbreviations for their bullets. For example; when you see GS in the *Speer* reloading manual it refers to their bullet line called the Grand Slam. It might look like this; "GS-SP" which stands for "Grand Slam-Soft Point". Other manufacturers have alternate designations for their own products too.

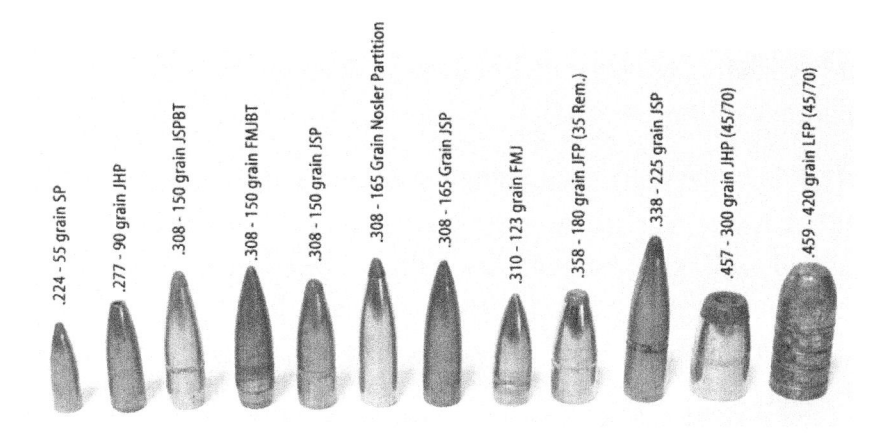

| Abbreviation | Explanation |
|---|---|
| JHP | Jacketed Hollow Point |
| JSP | Jacketed Soft Point |
| FP | Flat Point |
| SP | Soft Point |
| RNSP | Round Nose Soft Point |
| SJ | Semi-Jacketed or Short Jacket (SP or HP) |
| BTSP | Boat-Tail Soft Point |
| LRN | Lead Round Nose |
| HBWC | Hollow Base Wadcutter |
| BTHP | Boat Tail Hollow Point |
| PTSP | Pointed Soft Point |
| SWC | Semi Wadcutter |
| FMJ | Full Metal Jacket |
| Spitz-SP | Spitzer Soft Point |
| Spire-SP | Spire Point Soft Point |
| WC | Wadcutter |
| GC | Gas Check (lead bullets only) |
| FMJBT | Full Metal Jacket Boat Tail |

The list can be intimidating to the uninitiated so I'll try to simplify things a bit.

*Soft Point means the front of the bullet has lead exposed. These are expanding bullets for hunting game animals and (sometimes) varmints.

*Hollow Point bullets have a hollow point. This is accomplished different ways for different uses. HP rifle bullets are made by partially filling the bullet jacket with lead then squeezing the jacket to a point during the forming process. Match bullets (for professional target shooting) are normally hollow pointed because the points won't deform as easily as soft lead tips do. Obviously a deformed tip will hurt down range accuracy. Expansion isn't a concern for target shooters.

Many varmint bullets have hollow points but for different reasons. They are designed for rapid expansion to kill the critter quickly. Also, if you miss, the bullets self-destruct against the first object they contact. This reduces the danger of ricochets.

Hollow pointed hand gun bullets are made differently. They usually have an exposed lead front with a hollow cavity in the center. The hollow cavity allows them to expand more rapidly than a soft nose bullet. That's important in handguns because in my experience, bullets don't expand as reliably at handgun velocities.

*Nose shape may be either pointed, round or flat. Pointed bullets have a higher ballistic coefficient meaning that they lose velocity slower than flat or round nose designs. The velocity loss isn't great until you get beyond 100 yards. That being said there's no rational argument for using round or flat nose bullets unless it's in a firearm with a tubular magazine. If that's the case they are *required* because pointed bullets have been known to fire the cartridge ahead of it. Having five or six cartridges discharge in a tubular magazine is not something a sane person wants to experience.

*Boat Tail bullets have a taper on the rear of the bullet as well as the front. The purpose of the boat tail is to reduce drag on the bullet so that it retains downrange velocity better. It does work but the amount isn't significant until you get beyond 400 yards. Below is a spreadsheet showing the difference in drop between two 30 caliber, 150 grain bullets sighted in at 200 yards. As you can see there's very little difference until you reach the 400 yard range. If you're a sniper or long range rifle competitor the boat tail bullets might be worth the extra costs. Until then buy flat base bullets and pocket the extra cash.

| Bullet | Velocity | 300 Yard Drop | 400 Yard Drop | 500 Yard Drop |
|---|---|---|---|---|
| 150 gr. PTSP | 2900 | -7.9 inches | -23.5 inches | -48.7 inches |
| 150 gr. BTSP | 2900 | -7.4 inches | -21.5 inches | -43.7 inches |

As a side note here, the best thing about boat tail bullets is that they are easier to load into the cartridge. The thing to worry about is that, because they are longer than flat base bullets (especially in the heavier weights), they may not properly stabilize in some rifles and accuracy could suffer. You won't know that unless you try them.

*Bullet Jackets are usually copper. They will leave deposits in the barrel. It used to be that I didn't pay much attention to copper fouling but then I purchased a used firearm that was heavily fouled with copper. When I cleaned it with copper solvent I found that the barrel was pitted. I've learned since then that copper fouling can lead to corrosion and I've become more persistent in cleaning it out. Use copper solvent as regular part of your firearm maintenance.

*Bullet Construction is one area you'll want to consider carefully.

For many years the only options for high velocity bullets was the lead core/copper jacket construction. In most instances there's nothing wrong with that. I've used them for years with few problems. However, the two times I had problems gave me cause to look into some other options.

Your standard, copper jacketed, lead core bullet is made by drawing a gilding copper disk through successively smaller dies until it resembles a very small, (but tall!), cup. At that point the process varies somewhat. For years a precut lead cylinder was forced into the bottom of the jacket then the front was squeezed down over it. Unless it was a hollow point bullet there'd be a small amount of lead showing at the tip when the process was finished. The problem these bullets occasionally experience is what's called a "core separation."

When the bullet impacts the animal the soft lead front is pushed back into the bullet's jacket. This causes the front of the bullet to expand which increases its killing ability by making a larger wound channel. Sometimes if the bullet expanded too far too soon the lead core would completely separate from the jacket. Usually penetration suffered when this happened.

I've only had one time when the bullet itself clearly failed. It was when shooting a whitetail deer standing broadside at about 50 yards distance. The deer dropped like a rock but when I went to retrieve it I saw a large hole on the same side of the deer where the bullet entered. I'm used to seeing large exit wounds but this was the first time it happened on an entrance wound. Upon closer examination I saw that the bullet had literally exploded upon impacting the deer's side. I found fragments of copper jacket and the lead core all over the outside of the deer's chest area and nothing inside. What the deer died from was bone fragments from a couple of ribs that the bullet shattered. It didn't matter to the deer. Dead is dead but I never used those bullets on a game animal again.

Bullet manufacturers have addressed this problem several ways. Some actually hot bond the lead core (similar to soldering it into the copper jacket). Others have a ridge inside the copper jacket to lock the lead core to the base. Some manufacturers have gone to even more extremes.

For example, the Nosler Partition bullet has a double sided jacket. It's formed with a wall or partition in the center of the copper jacket with a lead core on both sides. The front can expand normally until it hits the copper partition while the rear half is held in place. They cannot separate so the bullet always retains a large percentage of its weight for deep penetration.

Other manufacturers are making a solid copper bullet. The front is a hollow point design to expand rapidly but it cannot separate from the lead core because there isn't one. The only problem with these (other than the price) is that copper is not as dense as lead so bullets of equal weight are longer than their lead/copper counterparts. Some rifles won't stabilize the longer bullets. You can compensate somewhat by shooting a lighter (therefore shorter) bullet since you don't have to worry about it breaking apart and not penetrating fully. Many lead core/copper jacket bullets shed 60 percent or more of their weight before coming to a stop. Solid copper bullets seldom shed over two percent of theirs.

Incidentally, most of my bullet separation problems seem to happen when the velocity was above 3,000 fps. In my big game rifles I've gone to heavier, slower bullets and keep velocities below 3,000 fps since then. I also use Nosler partition bullets when hunting elk with my 30/06. They're worth the extra piece of mind in my opinion.

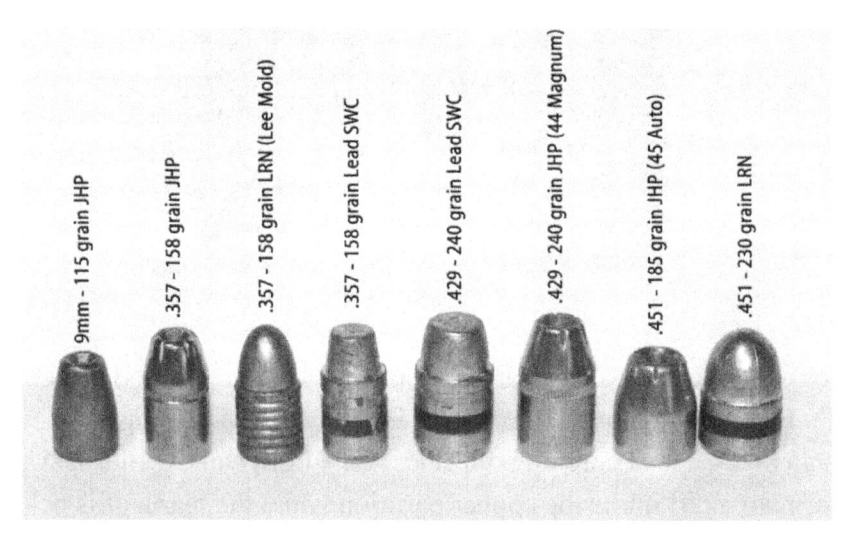

*Lead Bullets are made of lead and lead alloys without a copper jacket. They fell out of favor when bullet velocities rose above 2400 fps. (feet-per-second). Even the hardest lead bullets couldn't hold together at that speed. Lead deposits in the barrel were another problem. Also a lead bullet that was hard enough to take high velocities didn't expand well when used for hunting. Thus was born the jacketed bullet.

But lead bullets still have their place. They're used mostly in handgun bullets and large bore rifles from the black powder era. Lead bullets can be cast or swaged. Casting is easier in the home environment while most of the commercial manufacturers use the swaging process. There isn't much difference quality wise as long as the manufacturers and casters know what they're doing.

Lead bullets must be lubed to reduce bore leading. Leading occurs when lead from the bullet gets "smeared" to the bore and rifling of the firearm. Normally it's because the lead is too soft, the lube is not adequate and/or the velocity is too high.

Gas checks will reduce leading at higher velocities. A gas check is a small copper cup that's squeezed to the bullet's base during the sizing process. Its purpose is to protect the bullet's base from the hot gases generated when the powder ignites which reduces leading and makes it possible to get higher velocities.

Even with gas checks and hard lead alloys you're going to be limited to about 2200 to 2400 fps maximum velocity.

*Full Metal Jacketed (FMJ) bullets are used mostly by the military and hunters pursuing dangerous game animals in Africa. The military is required to use FMJ bullets by the Geneva Convention. They serve another function for the military as well. When a shooting a fully automatic firearm the bullets in the magazine are first bounced against the front of the magazine by the recoil then bounced off the back of the magazine when another round is chambered. Soft pointed bullets would be seriously deformed before it became their turn to be chambered and fired. Accuracy would suffer severely so the full metal jacket protects the integrity of the bullet.

FMJ bullets are used in Africa in pursuit of large, dangerous game. Most of those critters get a decidedly bad attitude about being shot and have the ability to do some serious damage to the shooter. Hunters and their guides need a bullet that's large and penetrates deeply to put them down quickly and permanently. Expanding bullets don't have enough penetration to do the job consistently so they use full metal jacketed bullets. Most of their firearms are at least .40 caliber so bullet expansion isn't a concern. Deep penetration is.

There's very little need for them in civilian life but sometimes you can purchase them for considerably less than expanding bullets. If you can get them cheap they make good practice ammo.

*Wadcutter and Semi-Wadcutter

Wadcutter bullets are just a cylindrical plug with both ends flat. These were created for shooting at paper targets because they cut a nice clean, round hole in the target. Paper targets are scored different ways. Sometimes you get the next highest point if your bullet touches the line and sometimes you only get the higher point if your bullet cuts the line. The difference is usually less than $1/16^{th}$ of an inch. A round nose bullet makes a ragged hole that's sometimes difficult to score. A wadcutter bullet makes a clean, well defined hole that cuts down on errors and arguments at the scoring table.

A hollow base wadcutter is just a standard wadcutter design with a hollow base. In theory, the base expands to grip the rifling when you fire the gun. It's supposed to be more accurate although if the bullet is sized properly the hollow base doesn't improve things much.

The long sides on a wadcutter bullet also provide lots of bearing surface so the bullet stays square in the bore when it's shot.

Wadcutter bullets are designed for low velocity shooting. They normally have a soft lead alloy and make excellent bullets for hunting small game. They're accurate and the flat nose hits with authority. The low velocity, poor ballistic coefficient, and soft lead slug make it safer to use in congested areas.

I've known people who liked them for home defense ammunition because they assumed the low powered loads and soft lead slugs would be less likely to penetrate walls and injure an innocent person in the next room or a nearby house.

A semi-wadcutter bullet has the flat front of a wadcutter only the diameter in front is less than the bullet's base. They're a popular style with handgun hunters who shoot lead bullets.

## Calibers and Bore Diameters

*Be sure you have the right diameter bullet for the cartridge you are reloading!* For example: The 7.62 X 39, the 7.62 X 51 NATO, and the .303 British are all *thirty-caliber* cartridges but the bullet diameter of the 7.62 X 39 is .310, the bullet diameter of the 7.62 X 51 NATO (308 Winchester) is .308, and the bullet diameter of the .303 British is .311. *These are just a few of the examples I could list.* Always be sure you have the right diameter bullet for the cartridge you are reloading! Don't just walk into the store and tell the clerk you want a box of 150 grain, 30 caliber bullets. Hopefully he'll know enough to ask for specifics but you can't count on that. Ultimately it's your responsibility to use the right components.

## Bullet Weight and Twist Rate

A bullet's weight is given in grains just like the amount of powder you're going to dump in the case. Bullets run the gamut from the diminutive .17 caliber weighing in at 20 grains to the massive .50 caliber BMG (Browning Machine Gun) weighing in at 750 grains each.

The weight must be proportionate to the caliber. Imagine a .17 caliber bullet that weighed 750 grains. It would be over 8 inches long. At the opposite extreme, a fifty-caliber bullet that weighed only 20 grains would be a flat disk. Its ballistic coefficient would be so low that it would have no stability in flight and would fall to earth within a few feet of the muzzle.

One of the other issues relating to bullet length is the rifling twist rate. The old muzzle loading rifles shooting round balls often had twist rates as low as one turn every 72 inches (1:72). In comparison, the twist rate for the .17 HMR is 1:9. The general rule is that longer, heavier bullets need a faster twist rate than shorter, lighter bullets in the same caliber.

Remington introduced the 244 Remington to compete (for sales) against the 243 Winchester back in 1955. Never expecting people to use it for big game animals they set the rifling twist rate at 1:12. It was very accurate with bullet weights up to 90 grains but accuracy plummeted with the 100 grain bullets favored by deer hunters so the cartridge/rifle combination lost favor with the public. Remington made some quick changes in 1958 (a faster, 1:9 twist rate) but the damage was done and they stopped production of the 244 Remington in 1962. In 1963 they introduced the 6mm Remington which is the exact same cartridge as the discontinued 244 Remington but the new rifles had the faster twist rate. It's still in production today.

The reason I'm bringing this up is because some rifles will not properly stabilize the longest bullets available in their calibers.

That's one reason to adopt a "middle-of-the-road" stance when choosing bullets.

## Making Your Choices

Bullet selection is critical to success whether you are talking defensive use or hunting (I'm going to assume that competitive target shooters aren't going to be reading this book). The guidelines I'll offer here are minimal.

Obviously if you are hunting large game (with a rifle) you'll want an expanding bullet.

There's really no reason to purchase round or flat nose bullets unless your firearm has a tubular magazine. Round and flat nose bullets will perform well when they hit but hitting with them at longer ranges (100 to 150 yards or farther) can be a challenge. Their poor ballistic coefficient makes them lose velocity (and energy) rapidly.

Bullets with a full metal jacket should be chosen only if you're loading ammo for the military or you're hunting large, dangerous African game.

Boat tail bullets are okay but the increased performance isn't worth the extra cost unless you're shooting at ranges in excess of 400 yards.

You don't need a controlled expansion bullet unless you're going after big, big game such as elk, moose, or bears. There's nothing wrong with using them on smaller critters if you want but they cost two or three times as much per bullet which is an unnecessary expense most of the time.

So for most big game hunting you're going to want a pointed, soft point bullet. Now you need to determine what weight it should be.

Again, these are my general recommendations.

For rifles 30 caliber and larger purchase soft point bullets that are just below the heaviest factory load available for that cartridge. For example, the 30/06 has factory loadings with bullets weighing from 110 grains to 220 grains. If you buy the 180 grain bullets you'll be okay for almost anything you can kill with a 30/06. I've used them on deer and elk with success. You could go with 150 or 165 grain bullets for deer but I've had the best results using 180 grain bullets on everything.

If you're using a caliber smaller than .30 I recommend the heaviest soft point bullets for large animals such as elk, moose and bears and upper mid-range bullets for deer size game. This would mean that with calibers such as the 270 Winchester you'd want to use 150 grain (heaviest commercial offering) bullets for elk, moose and bears and the 130 grain bullets for deer and smaller animals. If you're hunting in an area where both deer and elk (or moose) can legally be taken you might want to stick with the heavier bullets. A heavier bullet will work on the both, the smaller and larger animals but the smaller bullet might not do well on the larger critters.

I personally would not recommend using any caliber smaller than a .270 for elk, moose or bears. I've known people who've successfully used smaller calibers but they were experienced hunters and excellent marksmen.

In my opinion the 243 Winchester and 6mm Remington are minimal for deer and shouldn't be used on elk, moose or bears. I know people have used smaller rifles but again, they're usually experienced hunters (or just plain lucky).

Use lighter weight, hollow point bullets in any caliber when hunting varmints.

Again, these are general recommendations based on my experiences. It's best to go to the manufacturer's website or contact them directly to see what they suggest for each species.

Handguns

I prefer hollow point bullets when loading handgun cartridges. Due to my own experiences I don't have a lot of confidence that soft point bullets will expand reliably at handgun velocities.

When it comes to bullet weight use the same criteria as you do for rifle bullets. The bigger the critter, the heavier the bullet. We carry handguns primarily for protection against large predators (grizzly bears, wolves and mountain lions). In my 44 Magnum I use 240 grain jacketed hollow point (JHP) bullets or 240 grain lead, semi-wadcutters with gas checks. In our 357 Magnums I use 158 grain JHP's or 158 grain SWC/GC bullets. I can get higher velocities out of our magnum handguns by using lead bullets with gas checks than jacketed hollow point bullets. I shoot 115 grain hollow point bullets in my 9mm semi-auto.

Again, it's best to contact the manufacturer for specific recommendations based on your needs.

# Chapter Six: The Tools

Americans are tool freaks. Almost any metallic cartridge can be reloaded with nothing more than a steel washer, a powder measure, and a wooden dowel. Think about it ... the reloading process consists of depriming, priming, resizing, adding the powder, and seating the bullet.

You can use the hydraulic method to remove the primer: just fill the case with water, stand it on a nut or stacked washers with the primer centered over the hole, push a tight fitting dowel in the case mouth and tap it with a hammer to dislodge the primer. Next, put the primer on a flat surface, set the cartridge case on the primer (be sure the case is dry and centered on the primer) and tap the case down on the primer using the same dowel.

Resize the neck using a thick washer that's the proper diameter (size depends on caliber). Push the washer down over the neck to resize it.

Now add the appropriate amount and kind of powder using a premeasured dipper or weigh the charge on a scale.

Insert the bullet into the case mouth and you're ready to shoot.

So, if it's that easy, why buy do you need expensive reloading equipment? Because the right tools make the job easier and faster (and sometimes produce a better product).

In this chapter I want to begin with a section on portable reloading equipment. These are tools geared toward those who don't have room for a dedicated reloading area or they may be on the road a lot (like retirees in motor homes).

## Portable Tools and Equipment

Most people, by the time they're experienced enough at reloading to teach others, have a pretty impressive array of equipment. With a room full of equipment it gets hard to remember the early days using a Lee Loader and having only the bare essentials. I've got one die that perfectly illustrates the simplicity of the "old days."

**This is about as basic as it gets. It includes a full-length sizing die and bullet seating rod. With this and a way to measure the powder you have all you need (except components) to reload a 30/06 cartridge.**

My only regret is that they don't make these anymore. I bought this one at a pawn shop 40 years ago and I've never seen another one since!

The next step up is the Lee Loader. These are available virtually everywhere and are a great way to get started reloading ammunition. They include everything needed to deprime and prime the case, resize the neck, measure the powder and seat (and crimp) the bullet. I paid $23.99 plus shipping for mine in December, 2012. They do a fine job at a great price and everything fits inside the plastic case. Because they only neck size bottle neck cases (instead of full-length sizing) you'll only be able to use your reloads in the same gun they were fired in. You may also have problems with oversize cases in lever action, pump and semi-auto firearms. The good thing is that your loads will be light and case life should be excellent using a Lee Loader.

**The Lee Loader comes in its own plastic case. By purchasing the Lee tools for case trimming, chamfering, and a primer pocket cleaning you've got everything you need for reloading and case maintenance. And it will all fit in a shoe box!**

If you want to go the Lee Loader route you can get set up with everything you need to keep the cases in good condition very cheaply and need little storage or work space.

Photo provided by Lyman Products Corporation

Lyman 310 tool

The Lyman 310 tool is a very compact reloading system that's been around for a long time. You'll spend more for it than a Lee Loader but there's no hammering involved when you reload your ammunition. You will need a way to measure the powder. The only drawbacks are that it only neck sizes cases and die availability is limited to just seven different cartridges. It's on my wish list!

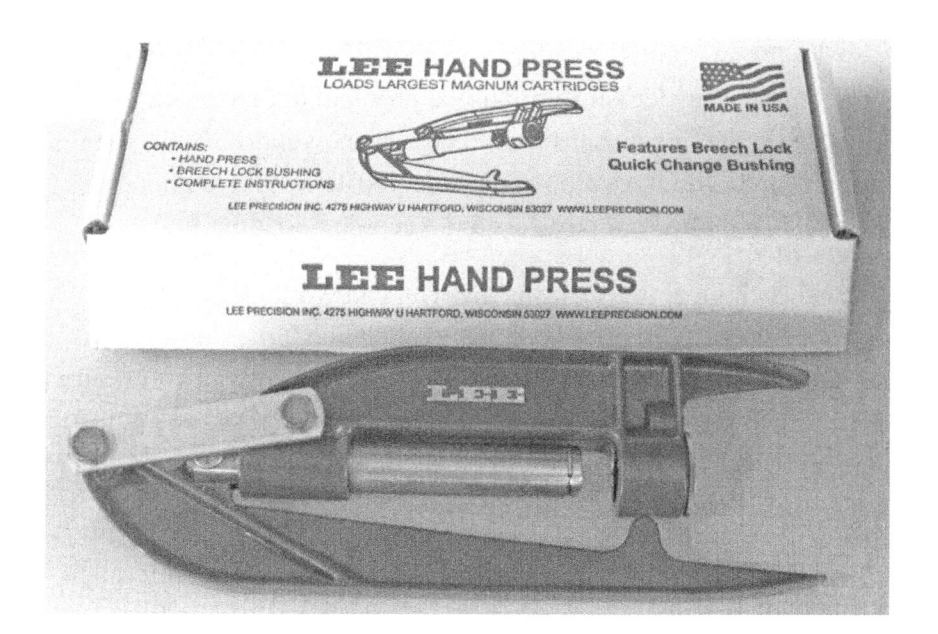

If you want convenience and the ability to full length size cases the Lee Hand Press is the next option. The price is reasonable and it uses any 7/8 X 14, die made for bench mounted reloading presses. It's a great option for those who don't have a lot of room or just want something that's portable. The only negative is priming cases. To use this press you'll need to purchase a separate priming tool.

## Powder Scales

Purchasing a powder scale is the next step up with any of these methods. While the dipper method will produce acceptable loads they're extremely limited in application. You'll have to keep loads at a minimum level for safety reasons and you're going to be stuck with one type of powder. You get versatility with a powder scale.

For example, my 30/06 Lee Loader only lists IMR 4064 for 125 and 130 grain bullets. But IMR 4064 is a great powder for reloading the 30/06. If I had a powder scale I could use the same powder for any bullets available for the 30/06. Finding a specific brand of gunpowder isn't normally a problem but I've seen times since 2008 that it was hard to find any gunpowder (or bullets or primers!). If you have a powder scale you'll be able to choose from a dozen different powders and keep on reloading bullets.

The other thing about scales is that you can work up higher powered loads. I'm not one to get excited about maximum loads for any cartridge. In fact, I normally load mine down a bit because it's more accurate, easier on the firearm and the brass lasts much longer. But I do like to experiment to find the optimum load for each rifle. I can do that with a powder scale.

Plus, the small digital scales will fit in a shirt pocket so you'll still be able to keep all of your reloading equipment in a shoe box.

Both digital and balance scales can be purchased for under $50.00. *Be absolutely sure that you use a powder scale that measures in grains.* A postal scale is not accurate enough for measuring gunpowder. One grain is equal to 0.0022857 ounces.

## Outfitting the Reloading Room

The previous section covered the tools available for the person with limited room. The major drawbacks to the options above are speed and versatility. If you want to expand your operation in either the amount of ammo you load or the variety of cartridges, you'll be better served with bench mounted equipment.

It still doesn't take a lot of money. At the time of this writing (January 2013), F. S. Reloading has three complete reloading kits for under $105.00 plus shipping.

You can also purchase items individually. The list below provides an overview of just some of the options available. I've included contact information in the Appendix if you want to do some research on your own.

## Presses

There are a lot of options when it comes to presses. There are single stage presses, turret presses, and progressive presses. There are O type, C type and, H type presses. (They look like the letter designation.) Some presses are made out of aluminum, some of steel, some of both.

A single stage press holds one die at a time. To use it you put in the resizing/depriming die then run all of your cartridge cases through it. Then you go to the next "stage" and set up the bullet seating die. It only does one stage at a time.

A turret press holds several dies on a circular "turret." You set up all of your dies in the turret and then rotate it to bring the proper die in alignment with the ram for each stage of the reloading process.

A progressive press is like a turret press in that it has all of your dies set up in a circular pattern but it also has "stations" for priming the case, loading the case with powder and putting the bullet in the case before seating it. (These operations are performed by hand with the single stage and turret presses.) With the progressive press you put an empty case in the shell holder then push the handle down. With each stroke of the handle the case is rotated into alignment with the next stage of reloading. When the cartridge is loaded it's rotated to a gate that lets it drop into a bin. Each time the shell holder rotates the case to the next station you place another cartridge case in the shell holder. Eventually there's a cartridge in each stage of reloading. At that point it ejects a loaded cartridge with each stroke of the handle. It's very fast.

Presses need to be built well to stand up to the pressures of resizing cases. If they are not the press will stretch and alignment between the ram and the dies will be off. "C" type presses are the most likely to have this problem but even with them it's seldom an issue if the press is well built. "O" and "H" presses are generally the strongest.

The other thing to look for is leverage. The more leverage you have the easier it is to perform resizing operations. Again, it's not normally a problem unless you're full-length sizing a lot of magnum cases or swaging bullets. If you plan on loading for the 50 BMG get a press that's designed for that cartridge. They're large, tough cases that will tax all except the strongest reloading equipment.

# Dies

The standard dies are 7/8 X 14 which are measurements of shaft diameter and thread pitch. You'll see some (mostly handgun cartridges) labeled as carbide resizing dies. The main advantages of these are long life and with some of them you don't need to use lubricant when resizing cases. The lock ring (or nut) is meant to hold the die in place in the press. Otherwise it tends to back itself out as you use it. Some models allow you to lock the ring in place with a set screw or other arrangement. This saves time when switching dies because once it's been set up you just lock the ring and then you don't need to re adjust the die each time you remove and reinstall it. You just screw it into the press until the lock ring makes contact.

There are a few specialty dies with different diameters than 7/8 X 14. These are usually for the 50 BMG and some large wildcat cartridges. (A "wildcat" cartridge is one that's not produced or sold commercially. These are often created to fill a "niche" in firearm/cartridge performance. Many common calibers - like the 243, 270, and 22/250 - were once "wildcat" creations.)

Every manufacturer extols the virtues of their equipment over their competitors'. I've used dies made by Lyman, Pacific, RCBS, Lee, and Hornady. They all served me well.

You'll see two, three and four die sets advertised along with factory crimp and universal decapping (depriming) dies.

Bottle neck cartridges use two die sets. One is the resizing and expanding die. The second is the bullet seating/crimp die. Straight sided cartridges need three dies. One is the resizing die. The second is the expanding die and the third is for bullet seating and case crimping.

Most four die sets include a factory crimp die. These are marginally better for crimping than the standard bullet seating die.

There are also micro-adjustable bullet seating dies. The difference between these and the standard seating die is that they have a rotating, micrometer type adjustment for precise bullet seating.

## Shell Holders

Shell holders are placed on the press' ram to hold the rim of the cartridge during the reloading process. In the "old days" the shell holder was machined into the ram. To switch to another cartridge you also had to change the ram. (I have two of those presses I purchased from a pawn shop years ago).

If you are using a progressive press the shell holders are round plates with cut-outs for holding the individual cartridges.

Many of the shell holders are interchangeable between cartridges. For example: the same one that fits the 30/06 also fits the 45 Colt Automatic, 25/06, 270, 308, 7X57, 8X57, 35 Remington, 6mm Remington, 22/250 and more. So if you reload those cartridges you'll need different dies for each but one shell holder will fit them all.

Lee sells a Universal Shell Holder set for $23.00 and up (depending upon your source). It contains the 11 most popular shell holders in one box. Individual shell holders are $3.00 and up so if you anticipate needing more than eight shell holders it makes sense to just purchase the set. I bought one for convenience. I used to have to sort through my boxes of dies to find where I left the shell holder (Let's see, did I reload 45 auto cases, 308 or 30/06 last?). If you purchase the set be sure to get the one for reloading presses. (The shell holders for their "auto-prime" will not fit a press.)

## Depriming/Priming

Most reloading dies have decapping pins built in. They do break the pins on occasion so keep some spares on hand.

You can also buy universal decapping dies. I have one that I use on brass that's dirty or gritty. In those instances I deprime the cases then clean them in the tumbler. After that I resize them. My dies last longer that way.

If you reload a lot of military surplus cases you may want to get a decapper from Lee. These are fast to use and very tough. The price is reasonable too. Just be sure the cases are boxer primed. (Look in the case with a flashlight.) If they're Berdan primed you'll have to use a different method.

Berdan primers will have to be removed by the hydraulic method (fill the case with water, stuff a tight fitting dowel in the neck and whack it with a hammer), or by poking a hole in it and prying it out. RCBS and other manufacturers make a tool for decapping Berdan primed cases.

There are a lot of choices for priming tools. I've shown three of my favorites in the photo above. The RCBS unit on the left is used when I only have a few cases to prime. It's a bit slow compared to the others but always starts the primers straight. It's my favorite for priming military surplus cases. The center one fits on a reloading press. It's manufactured by Lee and does a good job. I bought it as a replacement for the Lee hand primers I keep wearing out. The Lee hand priming tool on the right is my favorite. As I've said, I've worn several of these out but they're fast and provide a good "feel" when seating primers. Other manufacturers provide more options and they're worth looking into.

Most reloading presses come with priming arms. You can usually purchase tubes and other devices to hold more primers so that you can work faster. The only real complaint I have with them is that it's pretty easy to crush a primer when using a press. That long arm on the press has a lot of leverage!

## Case Lube

If you full length resize bottleneck cases you'll need to lube them first. As usual there are several options. I used a case lube pad. These are similar to an ink pad. You apply some lube to the pad then roll the cases across before resizing them. Each tube of lubricant will do thousands of cases.

You can buy case lube in spray form. Spray it directly on the cases or on a lint free rag and use it to wipe the cases. It gets expensive if you do a lot of reloading.

If you don't lube the cases they will stick in the die during the resizing process. When this happens you'll probably rip the case rim off trying to extract it. At that point you'll need a stuck case remover or you may be able to loosen the lock nut on the decapping/expander pin and screw it down to rem

You do not need to lube the case neck.

If you have too much lube you'll make "dimples
shoulder. If I see that happening I run a couple
through the die. This wipes out the excess lube.
though. If you do too many, the case will stick in the die. You should be familiar with the way a lubed case feels and be able to stop and back it out (before it's stuck too tight) when one *begins* to stick. The dies are supposed to have a "bleed" hole to let excess lube escape but it doesn't always work. Some are quite small and can get plugged up, (especially if it's been awhile since you used it last and the lube in the hole has dried out).

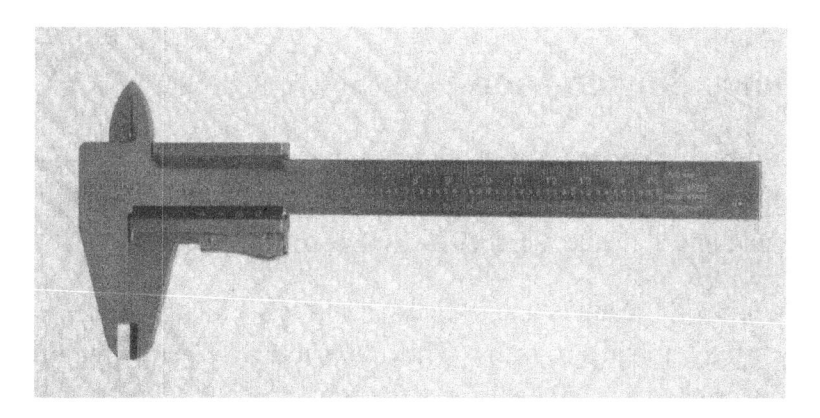

## Measuring Tools

Eventually, you'll want to get some measuring tools. The most versatile (and desirable) will be a set of calipers. Mine are "old School," vernier calipers and while very precise, are difficult to read (especially with old eyes!). Dial and digital calipers are just as accurate and much easier to read. The cost is reasonable too.

Case length gauges are another option. The best thing about them is that you don't have to look up the specs for a particular cartridge. You just use the gauge. It's a pass/fail tool though and

...rtridge you're loading isn't on it you're still going to need ...f calipers. I have one I got on a trade but I'd never fork over ...sh to buy one.

If you're not reloading a bunch of different calibers you should consider Lee case trimmers. You buy a cutter and lock stud first then the appropriate gauge/holder combination. There's no measuring involved. It's as fast as most other manually operated case trimming tools and keeps everything lined up properly so that the case mouth is trimmed square and every case is uniform.

Micrometers work great for case measuring but they're expensive and not worth the price when calipers will do just as well.

## Primer Pocket Tools

There are differences between a primer pocket reamer, swage, or cleaner. A reamer cuts the brass, a swage displaces it through pressure and a cleaner scrapes away ash and carbon deposits.

Primer pocket reamers and swages are most useful when you reload military surplus brass. They do a better job removing the sharp corners left on the edges of the primer pockets. (You can also use a chamfer tool.)

Flash hole reamers cut the flash holes to a uniform diameter for more consistent ignition. It's not usually a high priority with anyone except bench rest or long range shooting competitors.

Don't remove too much metal when reaming flash holes or (especially!) primer pockets. It's pretty easy to get overzealous and ruin the case.

Primer pocket cleaners merely scrape the residue from the primer pockets. Hard deposits are sometimes left in the bottom of the primer pocket after firing a cartridge. These can break lose and block the flash hole when you seat a new primer so it's a good idea to inspect the pocket and clean it when needed.

A small, flat blade screwdriver works almost as well for cleaning primer pockets as the tools specificallly made for the job.

## Powder Measuring Tools

Here the options include scales (beam type, digital or digital powder dispensers), dippers and dispensers (adjustable and bushing type).

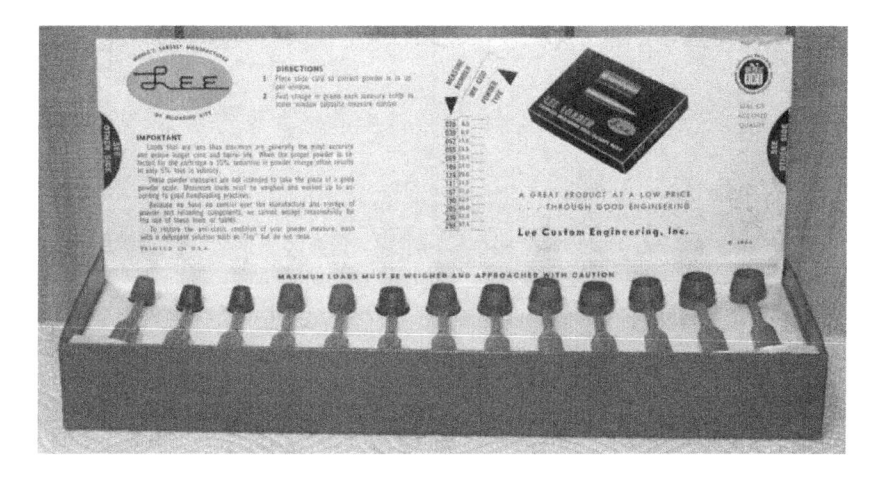

Lee Precision makes a set of dippers that will suffice if you don't want to delve too deeply into working up loads. They're cheap and fast. I use them quite often for handgun loads because of their convenience. I don't recommend them as the first choice because of their limited applications. You can't really work up special loads using them because the "gap" from one measure to the next is too large for fine adjustments. The other problem is that if you are working with maximum or even near maximum loads it's too easy to overcharge a case.

Bushing type powder dispensers have the same issues. They're fast and convenient yet also limited. I have both bushing type dispensers and the Lee dipper set and use them quite often (especially when loading handgun ammo) but I've also got a set of scales to use for maximum versatility.

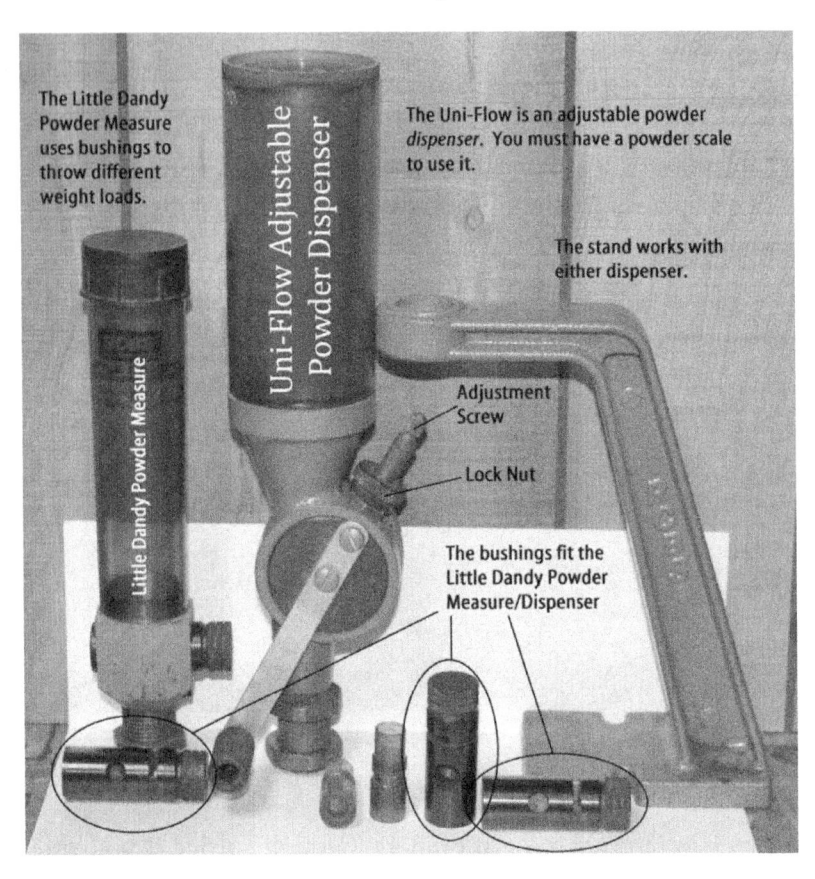

The Little Dandy Powder Measure uses bushings to throw different weight loads.

Uni-Flow Adjustable Powder Dispenser

The Uni-Flow is an adjustable powder *dispenser*. You must have a powder scale to use it.

The stand works with either dispenser.

Adjustment Screw

Lock Nut

The bushings fit the Little Dandy Powder Measure/Dispenser

Before I go farther let's clear up some things up. Powder *dispensers* do not measure gunpowder except in the most rudimentary form. Lee dippers and bushing type dispensers come with charts that list how many grains of "X" powder they dispense. *In a sense they both dispense and measure the powder charge* in the same way you use a measuring spoon to both measure and pour/dispense sugar. The problem that they have is that you can't really work up special loads using them because the "gap" from one measure to the next is too large for fine tuning.

Adjustable powder dispensers fill the gap left by bushings and dippers *but you must have a scale to use them.* Adjustable dispensers have been known to loosen or change position while you work. Be sure that the lock ring is tightened securely. I check every tenth load on the scale just to be sure everything is still where it ought to be.

The only way to fully meet your reloading potential is by using a powder scale. With a scale you can use maximum loads safely, use a larger variety of powders and bullets, and create loads for the ultimate in power and accuracy.

Scales are either beam type or digital/electronic. Both can be exceptionally accurate and the prices and performance are comparable.

The beam types are proven performers. They're calibrated by adjusting one pad up or down so that the scale reads "zero" with nothing in the pan. Once you have them calibrated you set the weights at the same number of grains as the charge weight then you just add powder until the beam is on the center line. Always check their "zero" before and after each session.

Be sure that any beam scale you purchase has the following traits:

1. It must have free movement without even a hint of sticking or binding. Adding even a single granule of powder should move the beam once it's near the center position.
2. It should have a dampening system. Many use magnets to dampen the scale. Dampening means the scales settle down and quit moving soon after you stop adding powder. If it doesn't you'll spend too much time waiting for the scale to stop jiggling so that you can read it.

3. It should be easy to read. That means the numbers and alignment marks must have clearly defined edges and be neither too small to see or too large for accuracy.
4. The adjustments should stay once you set them. You absolutely do not want them to change the setting by themselves!

Beam type scales need no electricity and they don't shut themselves off. Good ones are quick to use as well.

Digital scales are gaining popularity. If I was under space limitations I'd probably get a small digital scale. The big drawbacks are the need for electricity and automatic shut-offs. I'm not a big fan of battery operated gizmos. Some of it's our location and lifestyle. We live up in the mountains and it is a pain to make trips to town to purchase batteries. Plus, batteries invariably go dead when it's least convenient. We also live off-grid and tend to shun electrical devices if there's a good, non-electric option.

The nice thing about digital scales is that they're easy to read and use and some models are only slightly larger than a cell phone. Check the reviews for each scale. Especially the small ones. Some have a lot of complaints regarding accuracy

Most digital scales have automatic shut-offs to save the battery in case you leave and forget to shut it down. Just be sure that it doesn't shut off too soon. Otherwise you may spend more time turning it back on and recalibrating it than reloading your ammo.

The pinnacle of powder measuring tools are the digital powder dispensers. You fill the hopper, punch in the number of grains on the key pad and the scale automatically weighs and dispenses the charge. They are a bit pricey initially but by the time you purchase a scale and powder dispenser you may be spending almost as much as it costs to go digital. They're certainly worth consideration.

## Powder Tricklers

These are like primer pocket cleaners; nice to have but not hard to do without either. They usually have a hopper and a tube. You fill the hopper then turn the tube and powder trickles out the end a few granules at a time. It's used when weighing loads on a scale. You pour a measured, close to maximum, charge from a dipper or dispenser onto the scale then trickle on more powder until the scale indicates you have the proper amount of powder.

It's most useful when working up loads at ½ grain increments and when measuring maximum charges. *I do not throw maximum charges with a powder dispenser. I weigh each one.*

## Funnels

Funnels are indispensable and, fortunately, cheap. Lee Loaders are designed to be used without a funnel as are most powder dispensers. But once you purchase a scale you may as well get a powder funnel too. These are not like a regular funnel. Due to the miniscule openings on many cartridges it's impractical to make a funnel that fits inside the case mouth so a powder funnel's bottom is like a cone that sits on top of and over the cartridge case's mouth. They work pretty slick!

I do have a couple of household funnels used for pouring leftover powder from the dispenser's hopper back into the powder container. A large funnel makes that job go much faster.

## Cleaning

Case cleaning can be accomplished several ways. The simplest on a small scale is to use the Lee lock stud and case holder in an electric drill. Just put the stud in the drill. Use the case holder to lock the cartridge to the stud then turn on the drill while polishing the case with some fine steel wool. It takes less time to do than to tell how to do it.

If the cases are dirty, oily or grimy you can deprime them and wash them in case cleaner or soapy water, rinse them and then stand them on a towel to thoroughly dry them.

I use a vibrating case cleaner for large batches. These have a plastic tub filled with "medium" (normally ground walnut hulls or corn cobs and brass polishing compound) that vibrates, rolling the cases around in the medium. Depending on how tarnished the brass is it may take anywhere from an hour to a day to clean them up. They don't do much to clean the inside of the case but they can bring the outside to a high luster.

There are now ultrasonic case cleaners that use a liquid medium and ultrasonic sound waves to clean cases. They're a bit more detailed than other methods but clean the outside and the inside of the cases.

Cases should be deprimed before cleaning. I use a special depriming die or the depriming tool from a Lee Loader. If the case is dirty enough to need cleaning I don't want to run it through my resizing die.

## Trimming

Cases should be trimmed as needed. I didn't trim mine for a few years then I began having pressure problems that were traced to long cases. After that I bought a trimmer set-up from Lee Precision. It did and still does work great. Eventually I did some trading and acquired a case trimmer manufactured by Lyman. It's a little more versatile and it's faster than the Lee tools.

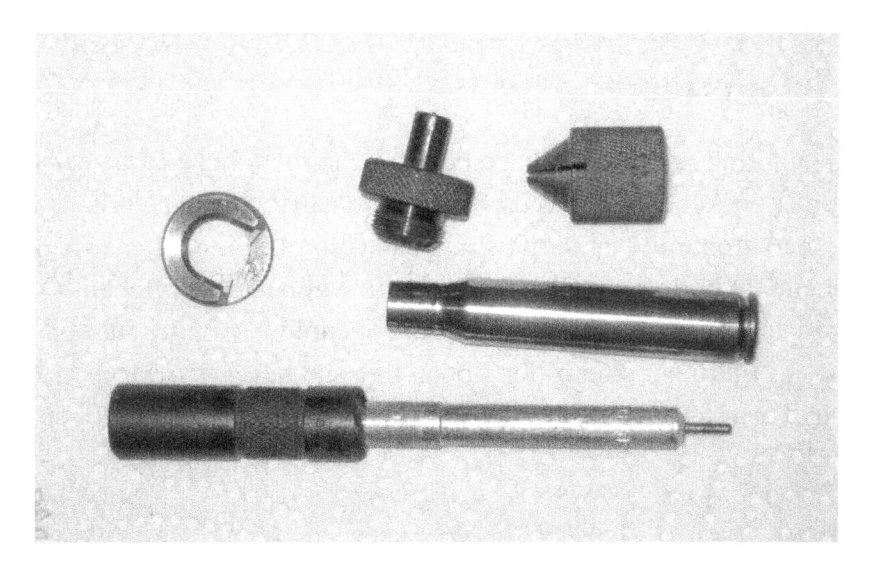

**Lee lock stud and cutter, shell holder and gauge, and chamfer tool.**

The cheapest trimmers are from Lee Precision. You buy a cutter and lock stud that fits everything then buy the gauge and shell holder separately for each caliber. They work great and take up very little space. I recommend them for everyone who purchases the Classic Lee Loader.

The next step up, are the manually operated trimmers from most major reloading manufacturers. These have a shell holder and a rotating shaft with interchangeable pilots. Again, the major draw with them is versatility and speed. One trimmer with pilots will fit almost any case. They're a trifle slow to set up each time so when I trim cases I'll do all of the cases in that caliber at one time.

Many of these will also thin the case neck with a neck reamer. (Neck reamers are sold separately.)

The next improvement is basically the same tool as above only it has a motor to make it spin. It's nice if you're doing hundreds of cases but the price is a bit high for the casual reloader.

## Chamfering

Chamfering refers to cutting a bevel or chamfer on the case neck or primer pocket edges. It's used most often after removing crimped primers from military surplus cases and after trimming a case to length. In both of these situations there will be a small ribbon of brass left from the crimp or trimming operation. A quick turn of the chamfering tool cuts this ribbon free and bevels the edges so that it's easier to start the primer or bullet in the case.

## Neck Diameter

I've mentioned the need for reducing neck diameter when the case thickens so much that it binds in the front of the chamber. I've never had a case last long enough for that to be an issue but if it becomes a problem the best tools are those that thin the case by cutting away the outside surface. That way the case thickness is uniform all the way around.

The other method involves using a reamer to cut brass from the inside of the case. In reality it probably won't make a lot of difference to anyone except a competitive target shooter.

# Crimping

I explained the reason for crimping in a previous chapter. Here we will look at the tools used. Most reloading dies also allow crimping the bullet to the case. Specific instructions come with the dies but generally there's a step inside the bullet seating die that squeezes the case mouth into the bullet's cannelure.

The regular factory bullet seating dies perform a "roll" crimp that's uniform around the entire lip of the cartridge case. It isn't recommended for use on straight sided, rimless cases like those used on semi-auto handguns.

Taper crimp dies squeeze the case tight against the bullet without rolling the case mouth in.

Factory crimp dies usually squeeze the case in at three different places.

All three work very well. The taper and factory crimp dies are acceptable for use on straight side, rimless cases that headspace on the case mouth.

Just remember, when you crimp cases you "work" the brass which hardens it and makes it prone to splitting. If the case necks begin splitting you might want to trim and anneal the brass.

## Bullet Pullers

Bullet pullers are for fixing "boo boo's" and for salvaging bullets. Sooner or later you're going to put a bullet in a case without powder in it. Then you'll face the dilemma of either pulling the bullet without damaging it or throwing the whole thing away. A bullet puller can save the bullet and the case for re-use.

If you don't anticipate pulling a lot of bullets you can pick up a kinetic (inertia type) bullet puller for around $20.00 or less. These are kind of a hollow hammer in which the cartridge case is held inside the chamber. You smack the puller smartly on a solid object (wood preferred) and the bullet falls from the case. At least that's the way it's supposed to happen. Usually after several hard smacks the bullet pulls loose then you have the bullet and powder contained in the chamber. You remove the case and dump the powder and bullet into a container. Now you can reuse one or both as need dictates.

If you're going to be pulling a lot of bullets you might want to purchase a collet type puller.

I bought a collet type puller when someone gave me a big batch of surplus ammo in 308 Caliber. I didn't own a 308 and the quality of the ammo was suspect (which is why it was given to me). I did own a 30/06 which could use the same bullets so I purchased a collet type puller and pulled all of the bullets for reuse in my 30/06.

A collet puller uses a metal case that looks like a reloading die body. It has a cone shaped collet with a handle on the other end for tightening it on the bullet. You run the bullet into the collet, tighten the collet on the bullet, then pull the case down and off of the bullet using the press' ram. It's relatively fast and does no damage to the bullet unless you over tighten the collet.

You must buy individual collets sized for the bullets you intend to pull.

## Loading Blocks

A loading block is a plastic tray with chambers to stand the cartridges in during various reloading steps. They're relatively cheap to buy or you can make one with a block of wood and an electric drill. It isn't an essential item but they're nice to have!

## Manuals

Either get a free manual online or purchase a print edition. I've put some links in the appendix but a quick internet search will find lots of places to download free loading data. Most powder manufacturers have free reloading information for their powders. There are other private sites as well. I sometimes print downloaded manuals and I keep electronic manuals on my Nook for portable reference material.

The Classic Lee Loader and many of the die sets offered by Lee Precision come with powder dippers and data sheets. If you compare their load data to the information published in reloading manuals you'll see that Lee data is always on the conservative side. There is nothing wrong with that. These are safe and effective loads that can be used in any firearm in good condition *as long as you follow their directions!* If all you want to do is reload using the powder/bullet combinations they've included they'll work great for you. But, if you want to expand your options all you need to add are a reloading manual and a scale. Then even with the Classic Lee Loader you'll have a lot more versatility.

A reminder on load data though: You may see some conflicting data between different manuals. This is because no two rifles are exactly alike. The results they post apply only to the firearm used in testing. You may get different results. That's why you should always begin with reduced loads and work up by .5 grain increments every time you change even one component.

## Chronograph

In the last few years chronograph prices have come down a lot! I purchased mine four years ago for $79.00 and I've never regretted spending the money.

A chronograph does only one thing: it tells you the velocity of an object that passes between its sensors. That may not sound too important but knowing the velocity helps you in a lot of ways. For example, another shooter wanted to run some reloaded ammo he'd purchased through the chronograph to see what kind of velocity he was getting. After the first five-round string we shot another string just to verify the results. The deviation in velocity from one cartridge to the next was often more than five-hundred fps (feet-per-second). That won't make a lot of difference in accuracy at 100 yards but at 300 yards with the cartridge he was shooting, there would have been ten inches difference in the points of impact between the fastest and slowest bullets.

The only way he'd have known would have when he shot at long range. Even then he may have blamed the inaccuracy on a number of things other than poor reloads.

My favorite load for my .338 Winchester Magnum has less than 10 fps variance between the fastest and slowest bullets.

Another advantage of a chronograph is that you know the precise velocity of the ammo you are shooting. The velocity shown in reloading manuals reflects the results for the rifle and load combination they were using. I can almost guarantee your results will differ. If you know the actual velocity of your reloads you can utilize drop tables to compute bullet drop at longer ranges.

The downside of a chronograph is that you can become a velocity freak. What I mean by that is that attaining maximum velocity can become your primary goal, plus, you get frustrated when your reloads don't "measure up" to published data. Velocity is only a small facet of reloading. In the past some of the most reliable and consistent performers were the 30/40 Krag and the .303 British. Neither is a "hot" cartridge by today's standards. Both have taken and continue to take every game animal on the North American continent. Don't get hung up on velocity!

A chronograph is probably not the first piece of equipment the novice should acquire but I'd put it on the "to get list" once you begin working up your own loads. If you take it to the range, you can charge a dollar a shot for other shooters to find out the velocities of the loads they're shooting. Let them pay for it!

Chronographs are usually available anywhere reloading components are sold. Check around a bit because prices vary.

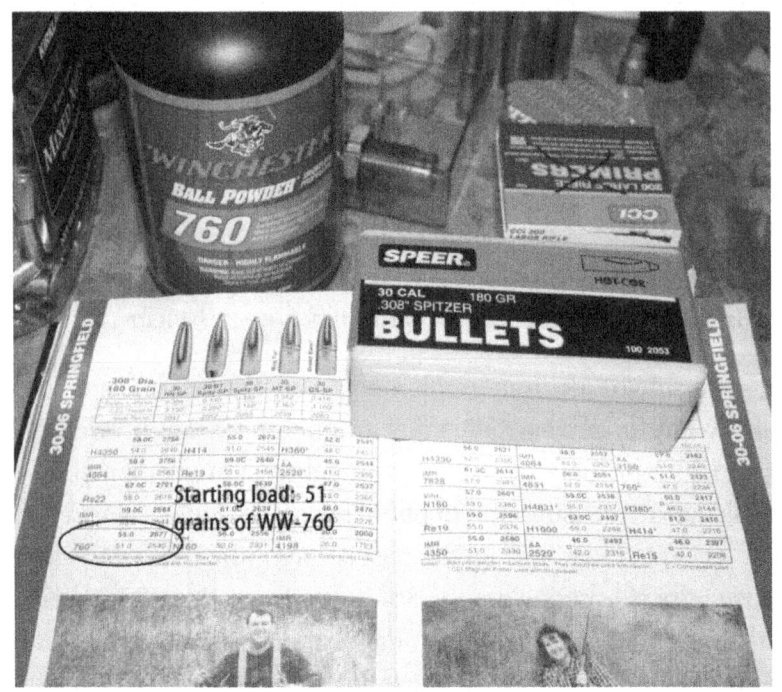

# Chapter Seven: The Process

Always follow the manufacturer's published loading data. When working up loads for any cartridge start at the minimum recommended (starting) levels and work your way up by ½ grain increments. If no starting loads are listed, reduce the maximum loads by 10 percent and start there. Do not exceed maximum published load limits.

If there are differences in the maximum load data listed in two or more manuals, begin with the lowest load data and work up by ½ grain increments until you reach your maximum safe load for that cartridge/firearm combination. Maximum loads are hard on firearms and the shooter (excessive recoil), shorten case life, and are seldom as accurate as reduced loads.

***Remember: any time you change a component you must begin at a reduced powder charge level and work your way up by ½ grain increments.*** Here are some things to think about whenever you change components:

*A three-percent rise in velocity requires a six-percent increase in chamber pressure.

*A three percent change in case volume (capacity) changes chamber pressure by six-percent. (Case volume can differ significantly between brands of cases. Bullet seating depth also changes case capacity.)

*Changing any component can significantly alter chamber pressure.

Your work area should be well lit and free of distractions, (especially when charging the cases with powder and seating the bullets).

## Again, watch for any signs of excessive pressure. These can be any of those listed below.

*Primer cratering (metal flows back around the firing pin hole).

*Difficult or sticky extraction

*Flattened Primer

*Expanded primer pocket

*Gas leakage around the primer

*Blown Primer (hole blown through the primer, usually where the firing pin struck the primer)

*Excessive or unusually hard recoil

*Head expansion

*Short case life

Some of these symptoms can be caused by other things but the only way to know for sure is to take the firearm, ammo and reloading dies to a gunsmith to be checked out. Until then, back off to a safe charge level.

## Purchasing Components

You should know enough by now to make an informed decision regarding the type and weight of the bullet to purchase. If you're using a Classic Lee Loader you can then purchase the designated powder for that load. If you're using a reloading manual choose a powder from those listed in the manual. Check to see if it requires magnum primers, if not then purchase standard primers.

So now you know the bullet, primer and powder you need to buy. The question is now, "how much of each?"

The answer to that varies. You're going to be somewhat limited in your choices because of the way things are packaged. Most gunpowder is sold in one pound containers. Primers come in boxes of one-hundred. Bullets are sold in boxes of fifty or one-hundred.

I like to purchase components in what I call "harmony." Here's what I mean: there are 7,000 grains of powder in a pound. Most gunpowder is sold in one pound containers so you divide the number of grains in the load you'll be using to see how many cartridges you can load with that pound of powder.

A favorite load in my 30/06 uses 49 grains of IMR 4064 powder with a 180 grain bullet. If I divide 49 into 7,000 I find that I can reload approximately 140 cartridges with each pound of powder. I'd probably buy two pounds of IMR 4064, three boxes (300) of standard large rifle primers and three boxes (300) of 180 grain bullets.

When loading for my .338 Winchester Magnum I'd purchase one pound of powder (I use 72 grains of powder per cartridge, 97 loads per pound of powder), one box of large rifle magnum primers and one box of 225 grain bullets.

When I have the money I may purchase more of each but I try to keep a balance between the amount of powder I buy in relation to the number of primers and bullets. I've also gone to magnum primers in my rifle cartridges. They perform better in cold weather and it can get very cold during the hunting season in northwestern Montana. I've killed both elk and deer when temperatures were in the sub-zero range.

You don't have to do your purchases the same way. I just find it more convenient to get all of my components at once.

Okay, you have a good work area, you have your components and reloading equipment and you know what danger signs to watch for. Now it's time to see how it's done! In the first section I'm going to show how to use the Classic Lee Loader. After that I'll go through the process again using a single stage press.

## Using a Lee Loader

Every Lee Loader comes with a dipper and charge sheet. Do not deviate from it!

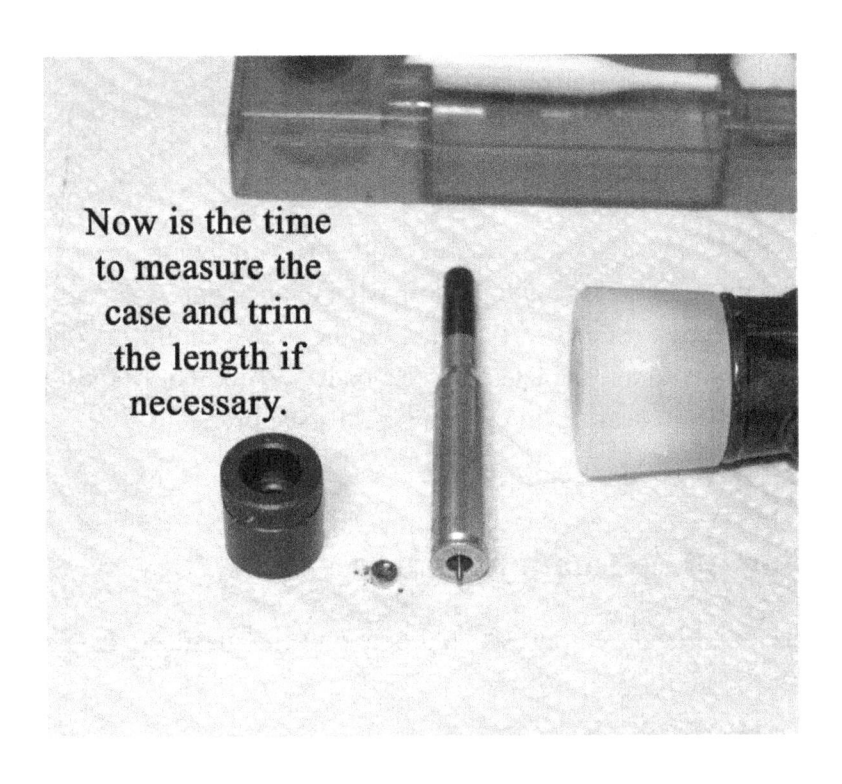

**Step One:**

Stand the case in the Decapping Chamber. Insert the Decapper into the case and tap the primer out using a plastic hammer or block of wood.

Now is the time to measure the case and trim the length if necessary.

*Step One*

Inspect and deprime the case. (*If the case needs trimmed do it now.* Don't forget to chamfer the edges after trimming the case. Clean the primer pocket if it needs it. If you removed a crimped in primer, chamfer the primer pocket before the next step.)

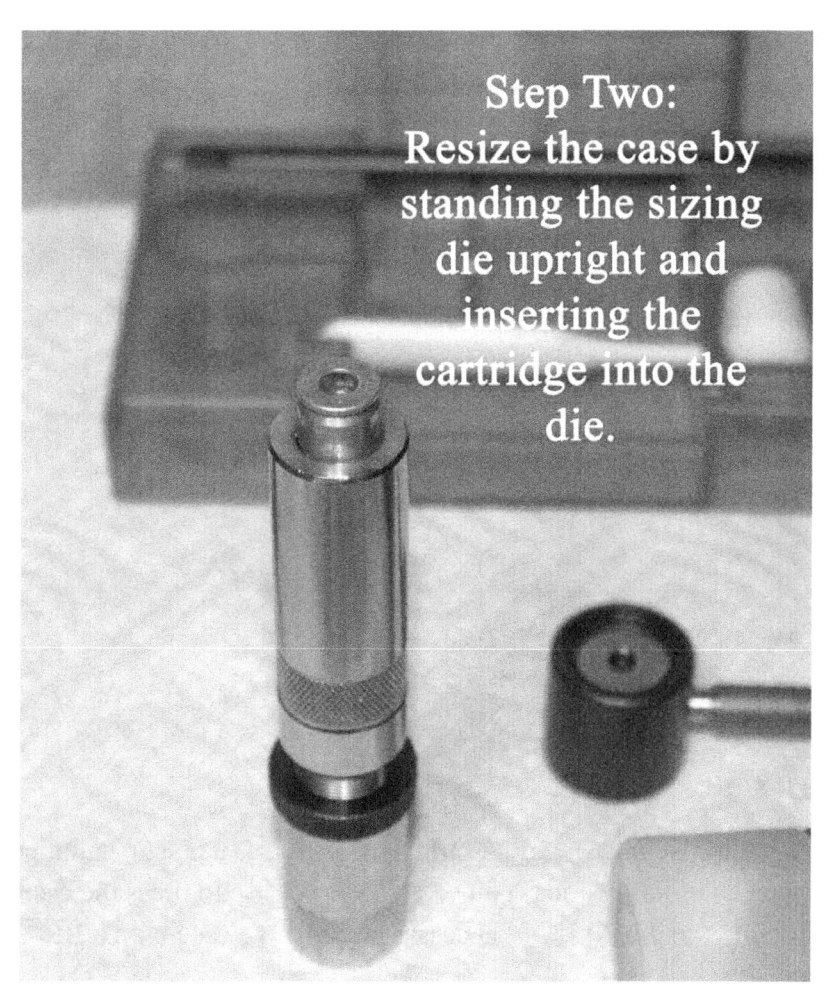

Step Two: Resize the case by standing the sizing die upright and inserting the cartridge into the die.

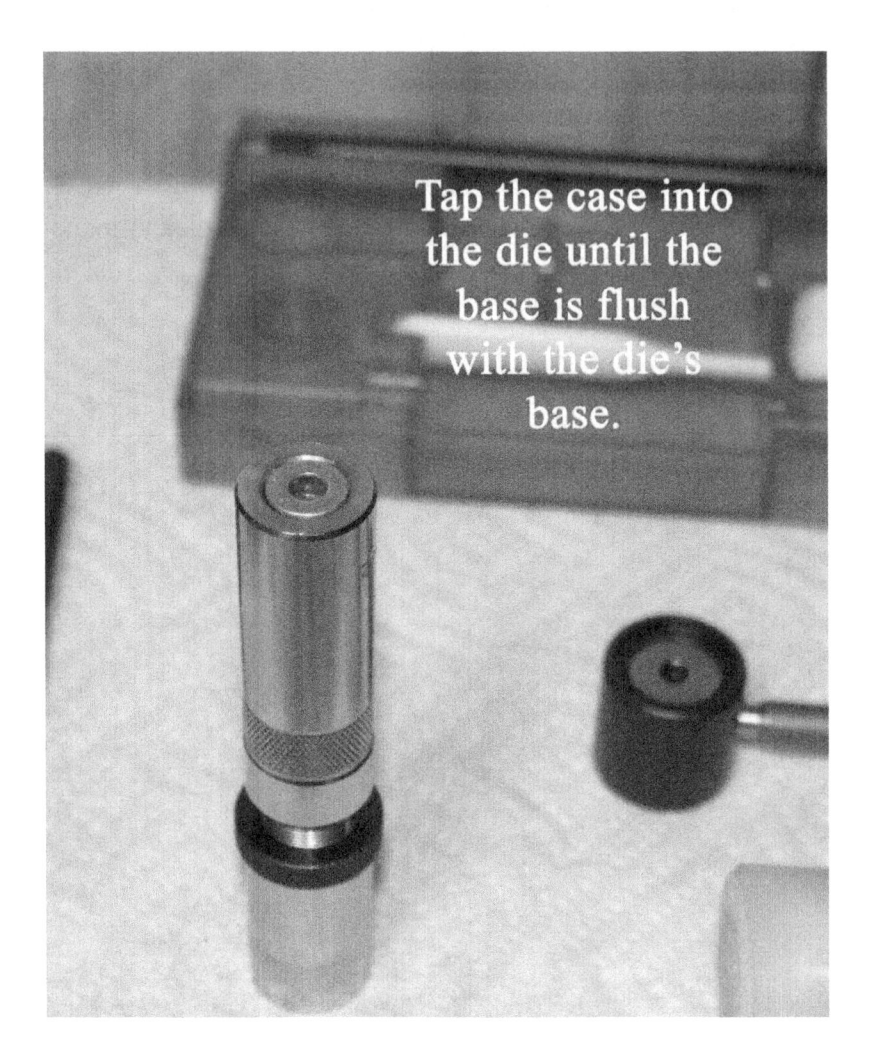

*Tap the case into the die until the base is flush with the die's base.*

### Step Two

Drive the case into the tool until it is flush. Use a plastic hammer or a piece of hardwood. You can also use a vise to press the case fully into the die. It is *not* necessary to lube the case with a Lee Loader.

Step Three: Prime the Case.

Put a primer (open end up) in the Priming Chamber.

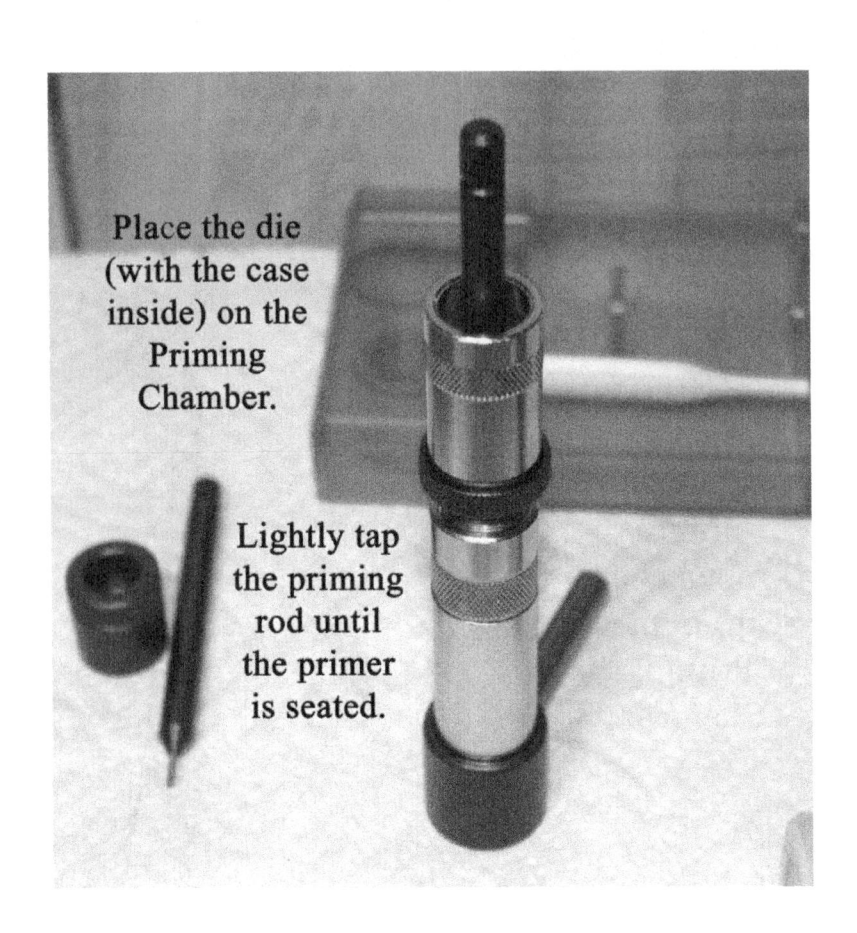

Place the die (with the case inside) on the Priming Chamber.

Lightly tap the priming rod until the primer is seated.

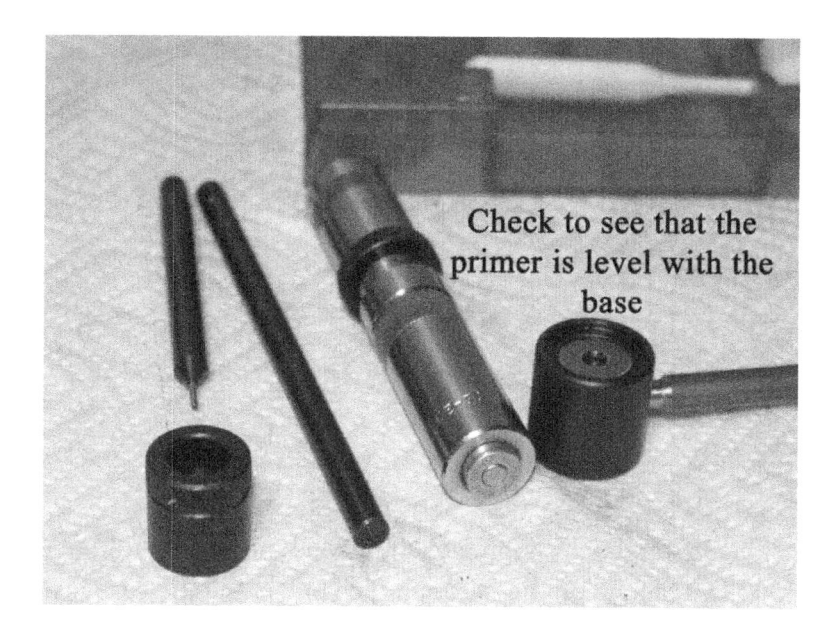

Check to see that the primer is level with the base

## *Step Three*

Place a primer (open end up) in the center hole of the priming chamber. With the case still in the sizing die, center the die inside the locater ridge in the priming chamber. The primer should be centered in the primer pocket of the cartridge. Insert the priming rod through the die until it rests on the bottom of the cartridge case. *Tap* the rod with a plastic hammer to seat the case down on the primer. Check to be sure the primer is flush with the bottom of the case. Keep the die pointed away from your face and body at all times. *Never seat the primer after powder has been added.*

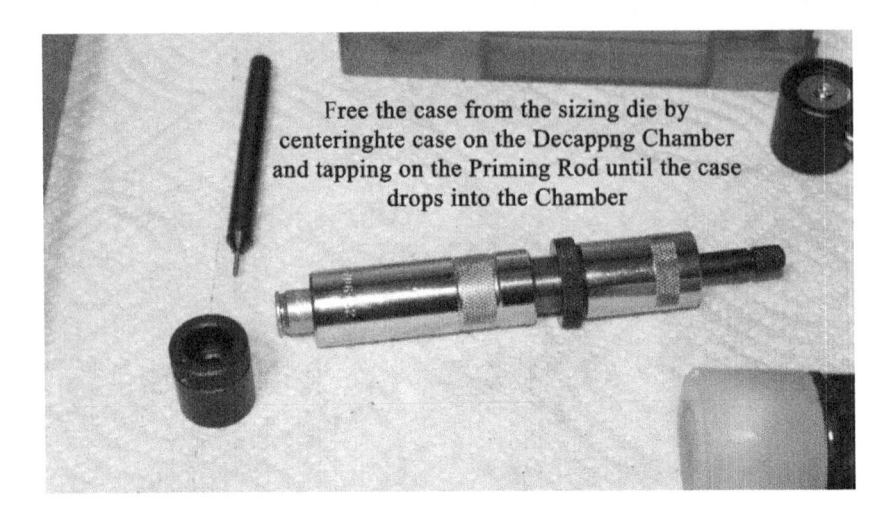

*Free the case from the sizing die by centeringhte case on the Decappng Chamber and tapping on the Priming Rod until the case drops into the Chamber*

Place the die on the decapping chamber and tap the rod to free the case. Leave the die on the decapping chamber and the case inside the die for the rest of the reloading process.

Note: If you've done this correctly, the case will be free from the die and resting inside the decapping chamber. This insures that nothing will contact the primer (setting it off!) when seating the bullet.

Step Four:
Add one level
measure of Powder.

## Step Four

Pour in one level measure of the correct type and amount of gunpowder. *Do not deviate from the loading data that came with the Lee Loader.* Compare the number on the dipper with the number on the load data chart to be sure you have the right powder measure.

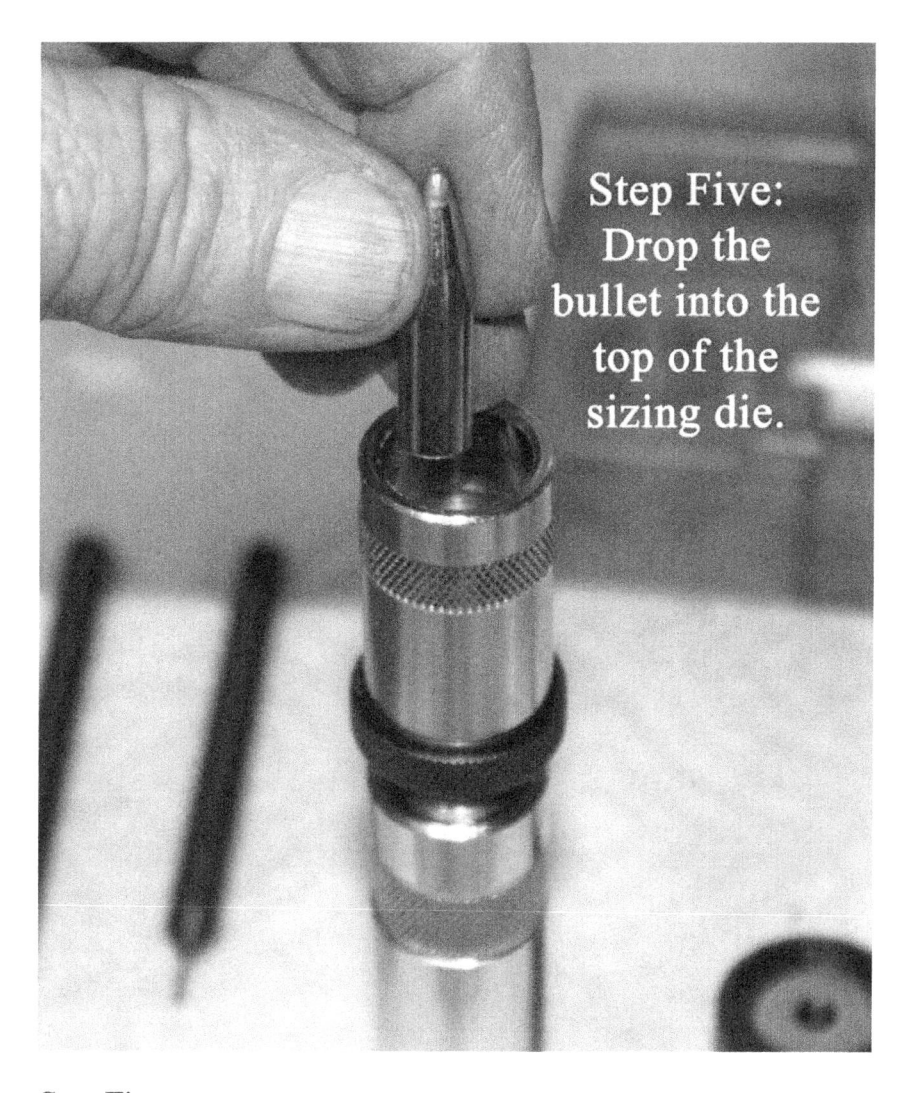

*Step Five*

Insert the bullet (base down!) in the die.

Tap the bullet seater in until it makes contact with the stop collar.

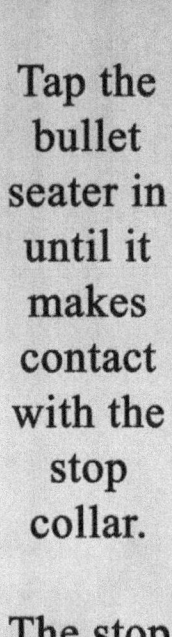

The stop collar must be adjusted up or down to seat the bullet at the proper depth.

## *Step Seven*

Insert the bullet seating tool in the die body and tap the bullet into the case until the seating tool contacts the stop collar. The stop collar is adjustable and controls how deep the bullet is seated in the case.

The easiest way to adjust the bullet seating depth is to begin with a properly loaded cartridge. Set the loaded cartridge in the decapping chamber with the die sitting on top of it as explained in step four. Now put the seating tool in the die and adjust the stop collar up or down until the seating die just barely contacts the stop collar. After that you can just tap the bullet seater down to the stop collar to seat the rest of the bullets.

If you do not have a loaded cartridge, proceed to step six. When you drop the bullet in take the die and lightly tap the bullet down until it's held in place by the cartridge's neck. Now measure the overall length of the cartridge and compare it to the number on the reloading data. If the bullet is not seated deep enough the overall length will be too long. Tap the bullet in farther by small increments until the overall length is correct. If the stop collar is set too high (the overall length is too long) you may have to screw it down to seat the bullet deeper into the case until the proper depth is attained. Once the overall length is correct, put the cartridge in the decapping chamber and die as in step four, set the seating tool in the case so that it's resting on the bullet and screw the stop collar up until it contacts the seating tool.

Another method (if your bullet has a cannelure or crimping groove) is to proceed as outlined in the paragraph above and seat the bullet until the top of the case is aligned with the center of the cannelure. You may or may not crimp the bullet in place. In most instances the overall length will be within limits.

Bullets that are seated too deep may be pushed into the case during handling (they'll also increase chamber pressures).

Bullets that are not seated deep enough will:

(a) Make the cartridge too long and it will not fit in the magazine or feed into the chamber properly, and …

(b) May allow the bullet to engage the rifling in front of the chamber. This can increase chamber pressures when the cartridge is fired and may also leave the bullet stuck in the barrel when the cartridge is extracted without being fired. If you don't notice the problem and chamber another cartridge it will most likely blow the gun apart when you pull the trigger. Let's try to avoid that!

### *Step Eight*

Crimp the case. (***Only if needed***.) Insert the cartridge, bullet first, into the top of the die body. Place the decapping chamber over the base of the bullet and tap it lightly with a hammer. What you're doing is rolling the mouth of the case into the crimp groove (cannelure). Check to ensure that the crimp is uniform all around the case mouth.

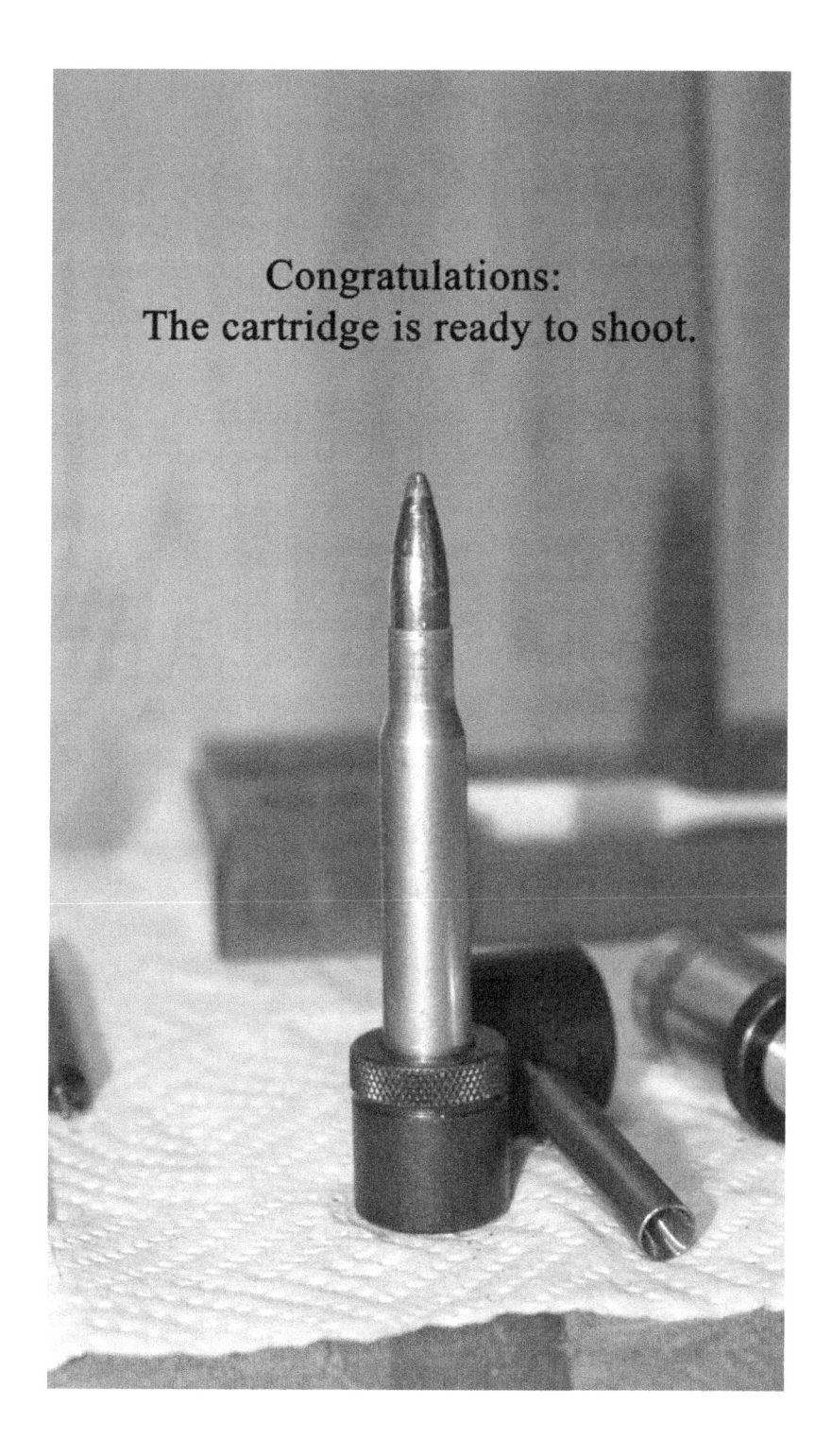

**Congratulations:
The cartridge is ready to shoot.**

# Reloading with a Single Stage Press

You're going to accomplish the same thing as you did with the Lee Loader but the steps are somewhat different due to differences in the dies. I'll point out the differences for straight walled vs. bottleneck cases in the text.

(Note on case trimming: I usually trim those cases that need it prior to resizing them. I'm not advocating that practice for everyone but it works for me.)

***Step One***

Install the proper shell holder in the press' ram.

***Step Two***

Install the resizing/depriming die in the press and adjust it. Follow the manufacturer's recommendation for setting up the die. Some recommend that you put the ram (with shell holder installed), in the "full-up" position then screw the die into the press until it contacts the shell holder. Next, lower the ram and screw the die in an additional one-fourth to one-third turn and lock it in place.

Note: In my experience this doesn't always work. I have two sets of 30/06, full-length sizing dies. One of them works great when adjusted according to the manufacturer's recommendations. The other pushes the case's shoulder back too far creating excessive headspace. The best way to check resized cases is by using a cartridge headspace gauge. I don't have one so I had to improvise.

The first indication I had that there was a problem was when a recently purchased used, pump (or slide) action rifle began experiencing cartridge case, head separations. The rifle was checked and the headspace was within specs so I began looking for other causes. I went through some range brass (cartridge cases picked up from popular shooting spots) I had and began running them through the rifle. Those that would not chamber were set aside for some experimentation.

I began resizing the long cases with the sizing die set so that it sized only the neck of the cartridge. I tried chambering the cartridge but the bolt wouldn't close. I screwed the die in another 1/4 turn and tried again. I kept that up until the cartridge would chamber with just a slight amount of resistance.

At that point I attempted to chamber the cartridge in my other 30/06. It took more effort to chamber the round. I screwed the die in another 1/8$^{th}$ turn and locked it in place. The cartridges will chamber in the slide action rifle with no resistance and in the bolt action with only slight resistance. That was good enough so I tightened the setscrews in the adjusting ring to hold that setting. Now all I have to do is screw the die down to the lock ring and it's all set to go. I just have to be sure that I use that die in the same press every time. (I have four presses.)

I ran another dozen cases through the die just to be sure that it was adjusted correctly before putting it away.

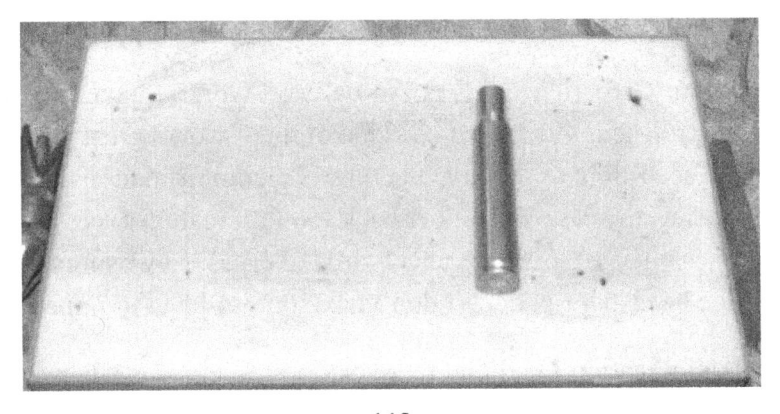

## Step Three

Lube the case. I've substituted a photo of a 30/06 case being lubed. In the rest of the photos I'm reloading a cartridge for my .357 Magnum. The carbide dies I'm using for this cartridge do not require case lube.

## Step Four

Resize and deprime the case by placing a lubricated cartridge case in the shell holder and running it up to the top of the stroke. Be sure to lube the case (if required). You do not want it stuck in the die! On bottlenecked cases it also helps to run a brush with case lube inside the case neck to reduce friction on the expander button.

At the top of the stroke you will hear a faint "ping" as the primer is punched out of the case. If the primer doesn't come out all the way you'll need to adjust the depriming pin. (See the manufacturer's instructions.)

Be sure to wipe the case lube off after resizing.

**Place a primer (open side up) in the primer ram.**

Place the case in the shell holder and push the handle down to seat the primer.

## *Step Five*

Prime the case and expand the neck.

### Bottleneck Cases

When resizing bottleneck cartridges the neck is squeezed under the bullet diameter on the up-stroke. On the down-stroke an expander button opens it back up to bullet diameter. This is necessary to compensate for different thicknesses of brass in the neck region.

While the ram is at the top of the stroke place a primer in the priming arm with the open end facing up. Push the arm into the slot on the ram and hold it there while you lower the cartridge case onto the primer. When the primer is seated run the ram up just enough to let the priming arm spring loose. When the arm clears the ram lower the case the rest of the way. The case has now been deprimed, resized, and primed. You're ready to add the powder.

Note: Some manufacturers use different priming methods. Always follow the manufacturer's instructions. I prefer to do the priming operation separately. See the section on tools and equipment for more ideas in this area.

**Straight Side Cases**

Straight sided cartridges use separate dies to resize the case and expand the case mouth. Install and adjust the sizing die by running the ram (with shell holder installed) to the top of the stroke. Screw the die in until it stops against the shell holder. Lower the ram and screw the die in another quarter-turn and tighten the lock ring.

You're now ready to resize the cases.

Note: some manufacturers deprime the case in the sizing die. Others deprime the case in the expander die. In either case I prefer to install the primer after expanding the neck.

Remove the sizing die when you've sized all your cases and install the expander die in the press. Adjust it according to the manufacturer's instructions. The expander plug opens the case mouth up to accept the new bullet. Most are tapered at the top to bell the mouth of the cartridge. Be careful adjusting it. You want to bell the case mouth just enough to start the bullet into the case. I usually have a bullet ready and adjust the expander rod in small increments until the bullet just barely enters the case.

Most revolver and some rifle cartridges will be crimped as well so you will be flaring the case mouth outward when installing the bullet then rolling it inward when crimping the case to the bullet. That's a lot of stretching and compressing in one small area. If you don't bell the case enough the bullet will crush the case when you try to seat it. If you go too far case life will suffer. If you don't crimp the case tight enough the bullet may loosen while shooting the firearm. If you crimp it too tightly you can deform the bullet and shorten case life. This is one of those places where practice makes perfect.

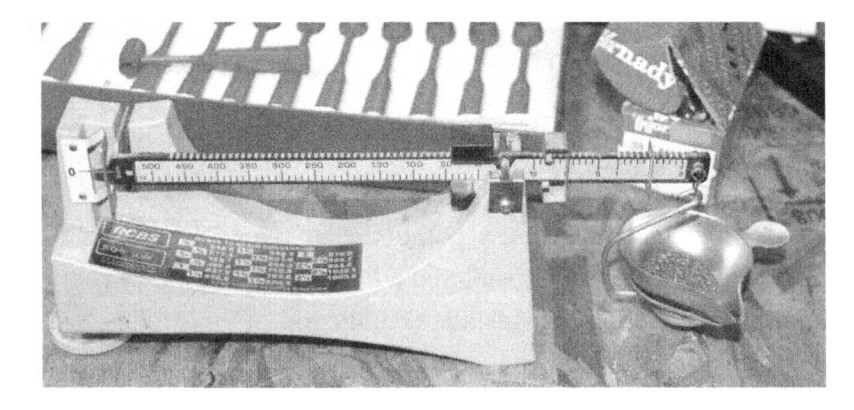

## Step Six

Now that the cases are sized and primed and the neck has been expanded you're ready to add the powder. Just remember: Be safe! Double check your components and the load data to be sure that you have the correct ingredients.

If you haven't worked up a basic load yet, do so now. I load one cartridge at the lowest listed load then seal it in an envelope with the appropriate information clearly written on the outside. If I can fire it then I'll do so and inspect the case for signs of excessive pressure. (My range is about 200 yards from my reloading bench.) If there's something wrong I'll recheck my data and ingredients. If it appears that I did everything right but the case is showing signs of excess pressure it's time to see a gunsmith. *Do not fire another round just to see if it really does have excessive pressure!* Remember to take all of your components and any other loaded ammo with you. You might also take the die and shell holder. DO NOT hide anything from the gunsmith. That's like lying to your doctor or lawyer. All it can do is get you hurt!

Assuming that the test cartridge looked good, make up another one using a different case, increasing the powder charge by ½ grain. Continue working your way up at ½ grain intervals as long as there are no signs of excessive pressure until you either reach the maximum listed load or you are satisfied with performance. If you begin having pressure problems stop and back the powder charge off one grain. That's your "basic load." Write the numbers down in a notebook or in the margins of the reloading manual so that you don't forget them.

If you are not satisfied with the load (perhaps the velocity is not high enough or accuracy is poor), try a different brand powder or bullet. Remember, each time you change even a single component you must start from the bottom and work your way up again.

When you are working up loads do not reload the same cartridge case each time. You may fire ten or more rounds just checking pressures. If you reload the same case over and over and over again you'll work-harden the case and your results may not be accurate. Use a different case for each test load fired.

Also, when I do this and I'm approaching the load level I'll be satisfied with I begin loading up three rounds of each test load and run some accuracy tests at the same time. Often your best accuracy will be attained a grain or two below the maximum load. By doing this I've often seen group sizes shrink and expand while I was still in the experimental phase. Now that I have a chronograph I use it as well, keeping a close eye on the velocity spread in each three shot group.

Remember, the velocities published in reloading manuals should only be used as a guide. Every firearm is different. Don't get hung up on velocity. Good shooting and accurate loads get the bullet on target. No matter how fast the bullet got there, a miss still results in an empty freezer.

***Step Seven***

You've measured the powder charge and poured it in the cartridge. Now it's time to seat the bullet. Put a resized case in the shell holder and run the ram to the top of its stroke. (Do not put a bullet in the case at this time!) Screw the bullet seating die into the press until you feel it make contact with the case mouth. Lower the ram. If no crimp is desired back the die off about a ½ turn. If you are going to crimp the case to the bullet, screw the die in an additional ¼ turn.

The next step is to adjust the screw that seats the bullet. (First back the adjusting screw off far enough it won't contact the bullet.) The easiest way to do this is to put a loaded cartridge in the shell holder and run the ram to the top of the stroke. Now turn the seating screw in until it contacts the bullet in the loaded cartridge.

The die should be properly set so take out the loaded cartridge and replace it with a charged case. Set a bullet on top of the case and carefully run the ram up. The bullet will be pushed into the case as it nears the top of the stroke. Once you've gone up as far as you can, lower the ram and check the seating depth of the bullet.

Measure the overall length of the cartridge and compare it to the data in your reloading manual. If the bullet is not seated deep enough the cartridge's overall length will be too long. Adjust the seating screw by small increments until the overall length is correct.

*If you are going to crimp the case on the bullet*, proceed as directed above but seat the bullet until the top of the case mouth is aligned with the center of the cannelure. The case crimp must be in the bullet's cannelure (sometimes called a "crimp groove). *Do not attempt to crimp bullets that do not have a cannelure.* In most instances the overall length will be within limits. Even if you are not going to crimp the case on the bullet you can still use this method to set bullet depth.

Bullets that are seated too deep may be pushed into the case during handling and they'll increase chamber pressures because they reduce case volume.

Bullets that are not seated deep enough will:

(a) Make the cartridge too long and it will not fit in the magazine or feed into the chamber properly, and

(b) May allow the bullet to engage the rifling in front of the chamber. This can increase chamber pressures when the cartridge is fired and may also leave the bullet stuck in the barrel when the cartridge is extracted without being fired. If you don't notice the problem and chamber another cartridge it will most likely blow the gun apart when you pull the trigger.

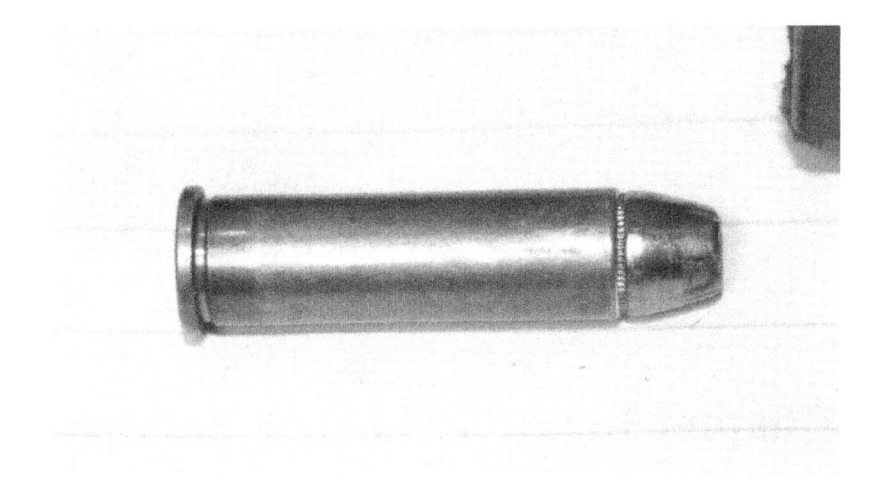

Once the bullet is seated in the case you are finished with that cartridge. It's time to go shooting!

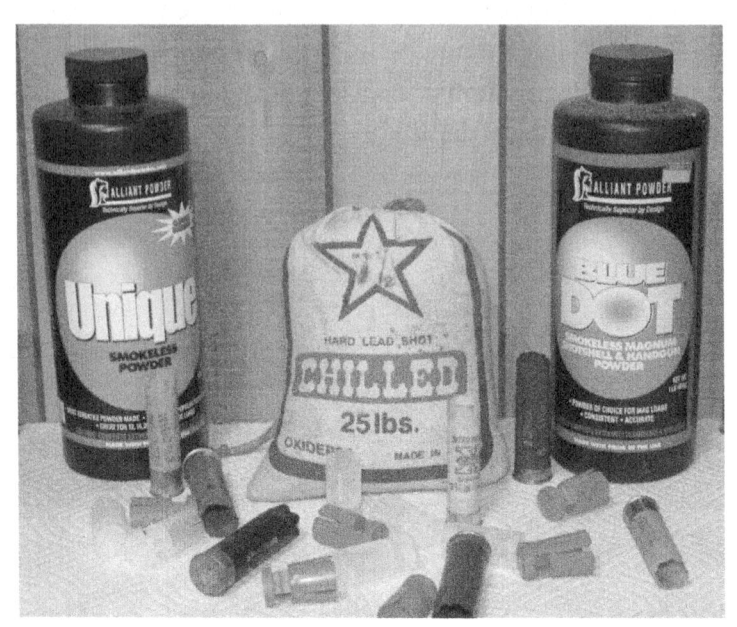

# Chapter Eight: Reloading Shotgun Ammunition

People reload shotgun ammunition for the same reasons they reload anything else. The savings in cash are similar to the savings you make reloading cartridges. The more powerful or specialized the load the more you save.

One notable facet of reloading shot shells is the diminutive .410. Store-bought shells for this little guy are expensive while reloading costs are lower for it than any other shot shell. If you shoot one regularly you need to consider reloading this little gem.

I may as well get a confession out of the way at the start of this chapter. I am not an avid shotgunner or an avid reloader of shot shells. I've been doing it for a lot of years but as long as the gun goes "bang" and the bird falls to the ground with something akin to regularity I'm content. I reload shot shells primarily because I can.

I have nothing against store bought shot shells. I just prefer to "roll my own." So, when you see my shot shell reloading press, try not to laugh! It works and that's all I ask of it!

I have Lee Loaders for both 12 and 20 gauge shot shells. I'm not as impressed with them as I am with their cartridge reloaders. They will however, produce functioning shot shells for those with a limited budget and/or limited space. Lee has stopped producing them so the only place you can get one anymore is if you find a used one somewhere.

I also have two, ancient, Texan shot shell presses. There's an interesting story behind those. My wife and I stopped in a pawn shop we'd never seen before and they had three shotgun reloaders on display. All three were old even then but one in particular caught my eye. Ancient or not, it would be much easier and faster to use than my Lee Loaders. They had price tags or $55.00 on each loader. I offered $25.00 for my favorite. He countered by saying I could have all three for $75.00. I wasn't too keen on the idea of having all three but I countered with an offer of $35.00. We finally agreed on $55.00 for all three. I went home wondering what possessed me to purchase three, used 12 gauge, shot shell reloaders when I only needed one.

When I went to set them up I found out that one was for ten-gauge shot shells. I don't own a ten gauge and didn't see a need to purchase one just because I could now reload shells for them but then the business end of this new revelation raised its head. I took some pictures, posted them on Ebay with a "buy-it-now" price of $85.00 plus shipping. It sold a couple of hours after being posted. (Hmmm, should have priced it higher!)

But, he was happy and I was happy so it was a good deal all-around. And, I still had two 12 gauge shot shell presses and $30.00 extra in my pocket. I wish I could find deals like that every week!

So, when you look at my shot shell reloader just smile like I do … every time I use it!

Reloading shot shells is similar to reloading handgun and rifle cartridges. You have the basic components of primer, case (or hull), powder, and projectile(s). Of course with a shotgun, "projectile" can be singular or plural. Shot shells also have an extra component to deal with called shot cups. (Wads went out of fashion decades ago for anything except muzzle loading shotguns!)

One of the major differences is that you do not work up loads for shot shells. Reloading manuals are very specific regarding the brand of the casing, primers, powder, shot cups and shot weight. There's no guess work or experimentation involved. In many ways that's a relief!

What you can (and should!) do is experiment to find the load that patterns the best in your shotgun.

In case you aren't familiar with shotguns and shot-gunning; patterns are different than chokes. The "choke" is a constriction in the bore diameter near the muzzle. In theory, the more severe the restriction, the tighter the "pattern."

Chokes are rated according to the percentage of shot hitting inside of a thirty-inch circle at forty yards. For example, if seventy-percent of the pellets (or shot) is hitting inside the circle at forty yards the choke is said to be "full." If the percentage is sixty percent it's rated "modified" and if only fifty-percent of the shot hit in the circle the choke is rated as "improved cylinder." If there is no constriction in the barrel it's said to be "cylinder bored."

What we need to understand is that poorly loaded shot shells can actually change the choke rating of a shotgun. To understand this let's take a look at "patterns."

"Pattern" refers to the way the shot is dispersed. A good pattern has the shot evenly distributed throughout the thirty-inch circle. A poor pattern may have "holes" where a bird or clay target could fly through that thirty-inch circle and never be touched by any of the shot that was fired.

"Hot" or the highest velocity loads are prone to scatter the shot more than lower powered loads.

Poorly loaded shot-shells may actually scatter the shot more, thereby reducing the density of shot inside the circle at forty yards. By the same token you can take a shotgun, experiment with some different combinations of powder, wads and shot and make it shoot a tighter pattern which may raise its choke rating.

The downside of reducing power is that you also lose downrange energy. Even with a tight pattern the shot must have enough clout to reach vital organs once it hits the bird. Like most things in life you must strive for balance.

## So how does one go about reloading shot shells?

First look at your equipment needs. Shot shell reloaders go through a process similar to cartridge reloaders. You must deprime, resize, and prime the case (or hull), add shot, a shot cup, then the shot, and finally crimp the case. Most shot shell reloaders have all of the priming/depriming, resizing "dies," powder and shot bushings and crimping "die" built into one press. Changing the powder charge weight and amount of shot are accomplished by changing bushings in the "charge bar." You can purchase single stage machines (in which you physically move the hull from one stage to the next), or progressive reloaders where you place an empty hull on the first station and the machine rotates it through each stage. Obviously you'll pay more for a progressive press than a single stage machine.

When you purchase a shot shell press find out if it will do all sizes of shot shells in the gauge you're using. Shot shells come in a variety of lengths from 2 ½ to 3 ½ inches long depending upon the gauge. You may have to purchase a separate press or a conversion kit for each gauge you reload. Find out how many shot and powder bushings come with the press. Some manufacturers include a selection of bushings. Some include only one of each. You may be able to purchase an adjustable charge bar. You'll need a powder scale to use it but it might save money over purchasing separate bushings for each load combination plus it will add versatility to your powder choices. Overall, be sure that your press will handle all of your reloading needs.

Lee no longer manufactures their Classic Lee Loader for shot shells. Their current offering is the Lee Load-All. These come in 12, 16 and 20 gauge and you can get a conversion kit to use the same loader for different gauges. The price is reasonable ($50.00 and up at this time) and the reviews are good. After reading the reviews I ordered one in 20 gauge. (Hasn't been delivered yet!)

## Purchasing Components

Before you purchase reloading components you'll need to decide what you want to accomplish. If it's shooting trap or skeet your needs will be different than if you were going after geese or turkeys. Where you hunt may make a difference as well. Many public lands ban the use of lead shot. That means you'll need to purchase components to load steel shot or one of the other lead shot alternatives.

Once you've determined your goals, open your reloading manual and see what components you need to purchase. (Note: reloading data is free from many of the online sources in the appendix.) You'll find listings as specific as powder brand and number, brand and type of hull (shot shell case), primer manufacturer, and even wad/shot cup manufacturer and number. Purchase the components you'll need.

You can do the same thing with shotgun reloading that you did with cartridge reloading. One pound of powder is equal to 7,000 grains. Divide the charge weight by 7,000 and you'll know about how many shot shells you can reload per pound of powder. Few shot shells use over 20 grains of powder so you'll probably get at least 350 loads out of each pound of gunpowder. Most shot cups are sold in bags of 500. Primers come in boxes of one-hundred and shot is sold by the pound (usually five or twenty-five pound bags). Divide the shot charge weight (in ounces) with sixteen (16 ounces equal one-pound) to determine how many pounds of shot you'll need.

## The Process of Reloading Shot Shells

Okay, you have your equipment and components. As with cartridge reloading you'll need a place to work with good light and no distractions.

Before you begin, inspect the hulls and discard those with cracks and splits. Knock out any dirt or debris. If you have a pressurized air system handy you can blow out the cases with an air gun to clean them. Unless they're made out of plastic you shouldn't wash them. If the outsides are dirty, clean them with a brush or cloth.

A shot shell press has all of the stations set up so there's no die changing. The major difference between a single stage and progressive press is that the progressive press has a plate that automatically rotates the case from one station to the next. With a single stage press the case is transferred to the next station by hand.

When loading metallic cartridges with a single stage press you deprime, resize and (sometimes) prime *all* of the cases *then* you switch dies before going to the next stage. When reloading shot shells on a single stage press you move the one case through all the steps before starting on the next one.

I've included a pictorial tutorial (I love using phrases like that!) showing each step of the shot shell reloading process.

**Before you begin** loading *be sure that your press is set up with the correct powder and shot bushings*. Refer to the loading manuals for the amount and type of powder for the load you want to build. Next go to the press manufacturer's data sheet showing which bushings you'll need to use to throw the correct powder charge. Find the right bushing and install it in the charge bar. Next find the shot bushing that dispenses the correct amount of shot and install it in the charge bar. If you have an adjustable charge bar you'll need a scale to set it for the proper amounts of shot and powder.

Be sure the hoppers are filled with shot and powder. I usually tape a note to the press listing the type and amount of powder and the amount of shot it's set up for. That way I don't have to start from scratch each time. (Since I have two shot shell loaders I keep one set up for magnum loads and the other set up for field loads. It saves time that way.)

Step One: Place the empty hull on the first (deprime and resize) station.

**Step Two: Push the press' arm down to resize and deprime the case.**

Sizing _____ Ring

Step Three: Raise the press handle to eject the resized case.

Step Four: Place a primer in the priming sation.

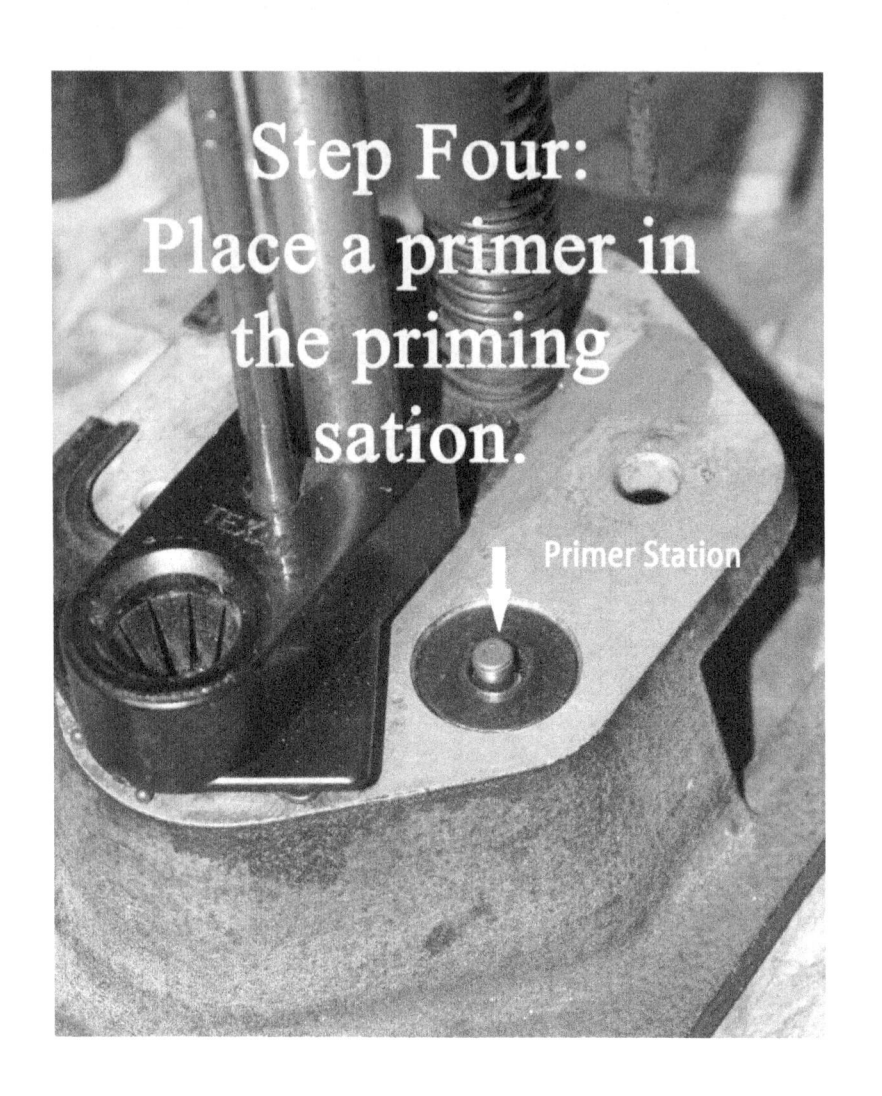

Primer Station

Step Five

Bring the press arm down to seat the primer.

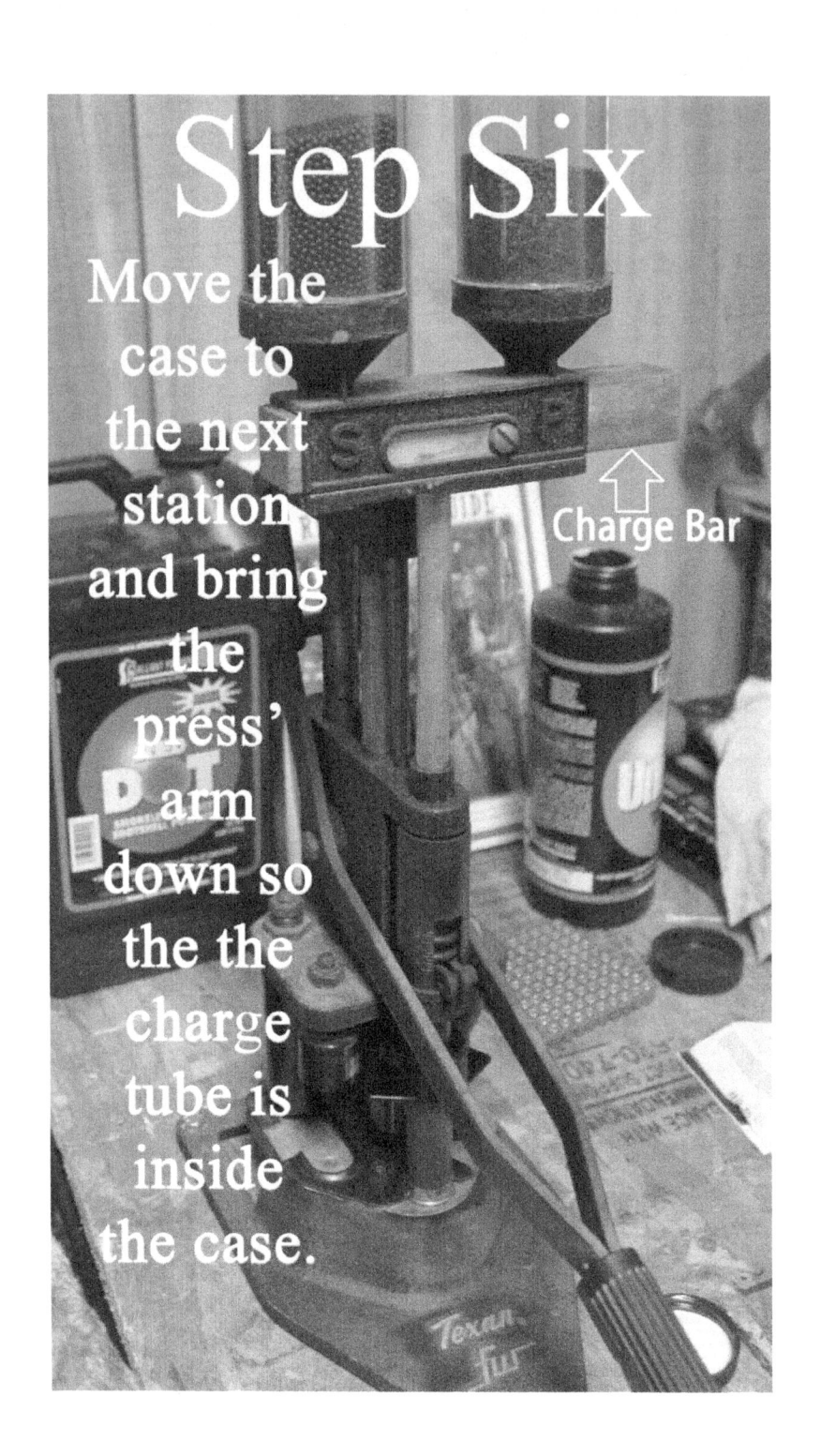

# Step Six

Move the case to the next station and bring the press' arm down so the the charge tube is inside the case.

Charge Bar

# Step Seven

← Move the charge bar to the left to throw the powder charge

# Step Eight

Raise the handle to the top then slide the wad guide over the mouth of the case. Start the wad into the guide then push it the rest of the way using the charge tube.

When the wad is seated in the case push the charge bar to the right to drop the shot charge.

# Step Nine

Move the case to the next station to begin the crimp.

# Step Ten

Lower the press so that the crimp starter can begin shaping the crimp.

# Step Eleven

This is what the case should look like at this time.

# Step Twelve
## Move the case to the next station

# Step Thirteen
## Run the crimp die down to complete the crimp.

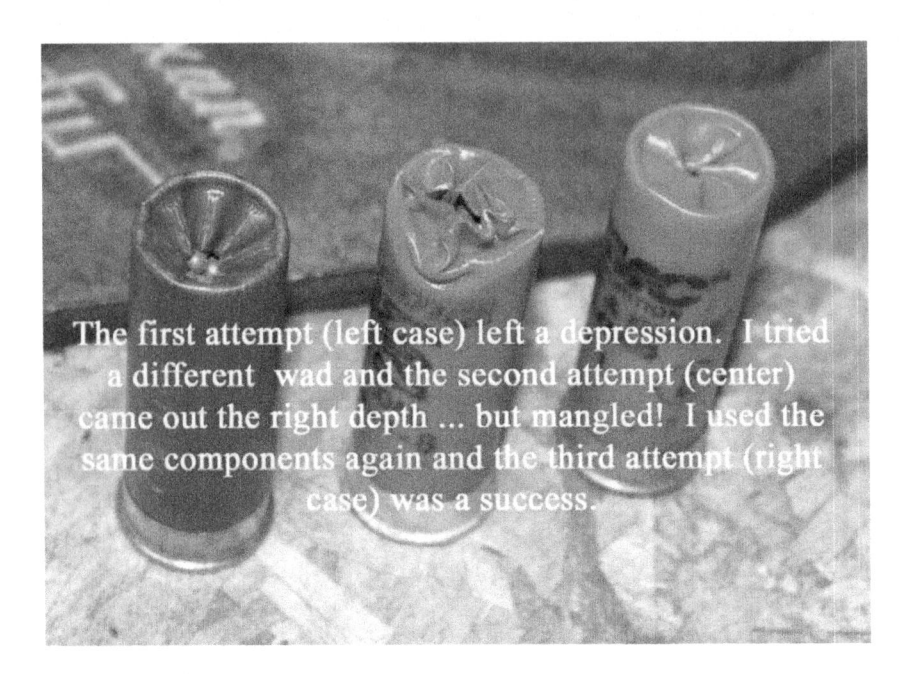

The first attempt (left case) left a depression. I tried a different wad and the second attempt (center) came out the right depth ... but mangled! I used the same components again and the third attempt (right case) was a success.

## Final Notes

If you're loading buckshot or slugs you'll need some different techniques. Buckshot must be loaded by hand because the shot has to be arranged in order if it's all going to fit in the case. Shot cups don't usually work either so you'll need the proper combination of over powder, cushion and card wads between the powder and buckshot. In some instances you'll need a "card" wad to place over the buckshot and a roll crimp to hold it all in place instead of the conventional "star" crimp. Slugs are loaded similarly to buckshot but you use a roll crimp without the over shot card wad.

If you're going to load buckshot or slugs be sure to follow the instructions in your manual.

You can get bullet molds for both slugs and buckshot if you want to try casting your own.

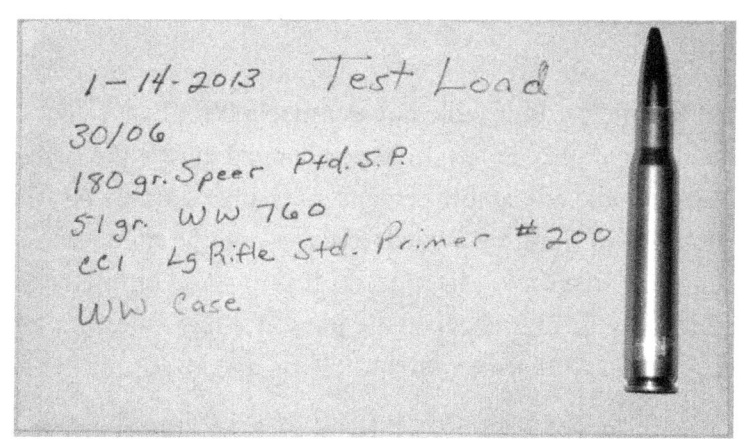

> 1-14-2013 Test Load
> 30/06
> 180 gr. Speer Ptd. S.P.
> 51 gr. WW 760
> CCI Lg Rifle Std. Primer #200
> WW Case

# Chapter Nine: Safety

I've stressed the need for safety throughout this manual so I just want to review a few of the points again.

Always follow the manufacturers' or the reloading manual's recommendations *to the letter*. No deviations or free-lancing allowed!

Any time you change even a single component or begin reloading that first cartridge: start with the lowest listed powder charge level and work your way up by ½ grain intervals until you (a) see any indication of excessive pressure, (then back the charge level off one grain), or (b) reach the maximum listed powder charge. This includes using cases manufactured by a different company. If there is no starting load in the manual, reduce the maximum load by ten-percent and begin there. (Review the signs of excessive pressure until you know them by heart!)

Use the exact powder listed in the manual. No substitutions allowed!

Sort brass and keep detailed (and dated) records of the load data (case, powder and charge weight, bullet manufacturer and type, primer and the number of times that particular case has been reloaded).

If you are using an adjustable powder dispenser, always check the last load thrown to be sure nothing's changed during the reloading process. I've had adjustable dispensers change settings between the time I began charging a batch of cases and the time I was finished. The first time it happened I had to start completely over. Since then I've always checked the powder charge in every tenth round. That way I discover any problems quickly.

Always recheck the "zero" (calibration) on your powder scale after you are finished using it. Sometimes scales get bumped or otherwise moved and the calibration may change at the same time. If it's off you'll need to dump the powder out of every case you charged since you last checked the calibration.

Never put gunpowder in a different container or mix it with other types of gunpowder. Do not use any powder if there's any reason to suspect it's not the exact powder recommended by the manual.

Do your reloading in a clean, well lit, environment that's free from distractions.

## Conclusion

This book is written for the novice reloader. As you gain knowledge and experience you can expand your horizons somewhat but for now be safe. Do not take chances. Get a good reloading manual and follow their instructions to the letter

Reloading your own ammunition is a fun and fulfilling experience but it's not something to be toyed with. Details are important. Consider this book the entry level course and keep studying. Most reloading manuals have sections on safe reloading practices. Read them and other literature on reloading.

One of the best books I've seen on the subject is *Modern Handloading,* by George C. Nonte, (available from Amazon Books). Don't let the publication date fool you. It's a treasure house of information on reloading, case forming, bullet casting and swaging and dozens of other subjects relating to reloading.

I've included an appendix with websites for reloading equipment and component manufacturers. I've done business with all of those listed. If I've missed a favorite of yours it wasn't intentional!

Enjoy your new hobby.

# Appendix

Lee Precision Inc. - http://leeprecision.com/

Dillon - http://www.dillonprecision.com/

Forster - http://forsterproducts.com/

Lyman - http://www.lymanproducts.com/lyman/main/

Hornady - http://www.hornady.com/

RCBS - http://www.rcbs.com/

Wilson - http://www.lewilson.com/products.html

Redding Reloading Equipment - http://www.redding-reloading.com/

CH – 4D Presses, Bullet Swaging Dies and Reloading Equipment - http://www.ch4d.com/

Machine for annealing brass. - http://www.6mmbr.com/annealing.html

Hornady Manufacturing Ballistic Tables - http://www.hornady.com/assets/files/ballistics/2012CatalogCenterSpread.pdf

Alliant Powder - http://www.alliantpowder.com/default.aspx

Hodgdon Powder (also IMR Rifle Powder) - http://www.hodgdon.com/index.html

Winchester Western Powder - http://www.wwpowder.com/history.html

IMR Gun Powder Website - http://www.imrpowder.com/

Accurate Reloading Powder - http://www.accuratepowder.com/

Reloading Pages of M. D. Smith - http://www.reloadammo.com/

Speer Bullets - http://www.speer-bullets.com/default.aspx

Nosler Bullets - http://www.nosler.com/

Barnes Bullets - http://www.barnesbullets.com/

Brownells – Reloading and gunsmith supplies. - http://www.brownells.com/

FS Reloading Supplies - https://fsreloading.com/

Midway U. S. A. - http://www.midwayusa.com/

Midsouth Shooter's Supply - http://www.midsouthshooterssupply.com/

Cabelas Outdoor Supplies - http://www.cabelas.com/

\*\*\*\*\*\*\*\*\*\*\*\*\*\*\*\*\*\*\*\*\*\*\*\*\*

Now that you've finished this book check out some of the other titles written by this author.

**Creating the Low-Budget Homestead**
Steven D. Gregersen

If you've ever thought about pursuing a self-sufficient lifestyle on your own rural homestead or survival retreat but feared you didn't have the money or skills to do it, you simply must read this book. It is a goldmine of practical steps and instructions to take you from dreaming about an off-grid, independent lifestyle to living one!

There are hundreds of things to think about before planning and starting your new life, and this book will save you valuable time and money by steering you down productive paths and making you carefully consider others. Just some of the areas it covers include:

- 4 rules for defining your goals for your homestead or retreat
- creative ways to find inexpensive rural property to buy
- the essential tools, vehicles, and skills you will need to succeed
- 10 rules for a self-sufficient garden
- designing the off-grid home so it's warm in winter and cool in summer
- questions you must ask before investing in farm animals, livestock, or even pets
- 9 rules for getting along with your country neighbors
- tips for working smart, being realistic, and avoiding burnout

A person who's reliant on others for the necessities of life will always be subject to the people, companies, and agencies who feed, house, and protect him. With determination, creativity, and the knowledge in this book, you can break this cycle of dependence and become a successful low-budget homesteader!

Creating the Low-Budget Homestead or retreat is available from Paladin Press and Amazon Books, or you can get a copy signed by the author for $25.00 (postage paid in the continental United States) by emailing him at: creatingthelowbudgethomestead@gmail.com.

For information regarding other books written by the author or his wife go to his website at povertyprepper.net or visit his blog at http://livinglifeoffgrid.blogspot.com/. The blog is a journal of their life as off-grid homesteaders in northwestern Montana.

The author's wife keeps a blog at http://povertyprepping.blogspot.com/. In it you'll find information regarding low-budget ways to stock up and prepare food for emergencies. She also has information regarding other books she's published. I invite you to peruse her blog and her website at povertyprepper.com.